Library of
Davidson College

Beyond the Electoral Connection

BEYOND

KIM EZRA SHIENBAUM

THE ELECTORAL CONNECTION

A Reassessment
of the Role of Voting
in Contemporary
American Politics

UNIVERSITY OF PENNSYLVANIA PRESS
Philadelphia

To my Mother

The table on page 36 is reprinted by permission of Dow Jones & Company, Inc., from Lloyd N. Cutler and C. Douglas Dillon, "Can We Improve Our Constitutional System?" *Wall Street Journal*, February 15, 1983, p. 32. Copyright © Dow Jones & Company, Inc., 1983. All Rights Reserved.

Copyright © 1984 by the University of Pennsylvania Press
All rights reserved

Library of Congress Cataloging in Publication Data

Shienbaum, Kim Ezra.
   Beyond the electoral connection.
   Includes index.
   1. Elections—United States. 2. Voting—United States.
3. Political participation—United States. I. Title.
JK1967.S55 1984   324.973'092   83-14485
ISBN 0-8122-7916-6

Printed in the United States of America

Contents

Preface vii

ONE
Who Votes and Why: A Critical Look at the Consensus and Revisionist Views 1

TWO
Voting as an Act of Political Ritualism 16

Voter Adjustments to the Electoral Process 18
Do Voters Make Prospective Choices? 18
The Disintegration of Parties in the Electoral Process 23
Do Voters Make Retrospective Judgments? 35

THREE
Extra-Electoral Participatory Activity 44

The Makers of Public Policy 45

The Diminishing Roles of Congress and the President 46

The Expanding Roles of the Bureaucracy and the Courts 53

The Political Role of the Bureaucracy 54
The Political Role of the Supreme Court 58

The Changing Means of Popular Influence and Control 62

Popular Influence at the Administrative Level 67
Popular Influence at the Judicial Level 70

The Changing Means of Popular Control 72
Class Bias in Political Participation and Voting 76

Four
The Symbolism of Elections and the Ritualism of Voting 83

Who Votes—The Variables 84
Why People Vote 95

Five
The Role of Elections in American Democracy 110

The Origins of Representative Democracy 111
Is the United States a Representative Democracy? 114
The United States: A "Citizen-Participant" Democracy 116
Can Nonelectoral Policy-making Be Curtailed? 118
Elections as Rituals 123
The Role of Elections in a "Citizen-Participant" Democracy 127

Index 133

Preface

American voting behavior has long been paradoxical. Empirical analyses over the past thirty years have revealed that voting choices, in general, are made noninstrumentally by voters who tend to be citizens with the highest levels of education, income, and political experience—and who profess to hold the electoral process in the highest regard. Why then are "smart folks voting dumb"?

This book reassesses the role of voting within the context of the operative realities of contemporary American politics. We hope to explain not only the socioeconomic bias but also the noninstrumentality of American voting behavior in terms that reaffirm the rationality of U.S. citizens.

We will explore the vitiation of the cultural, institutional, and organizational underpinnings of representative democracy and examine the effects of the de facto transfer of decision-making responsibilities in several important areas to the processes of judicial and bureaucratic politics rather than electoral politics. The core of this effort is the contention that developmental changes, both within and outside of the electoral process, have altered the nature of American democracy in fundamental ways—ways that have made voting the least, rather than the most, important participatory resource.

This study does not pretend to break new empirical ground. Others have seen to it that those fields have been well tilled, and we intend to make full use of the fruits of their labors. Instead, this book attempts to reconceptualize and reinterpret an important aspect of American political behavior whose contradictions have long puzzled informed observers both here and abroad. It offers readers an alternative and, we hope, controversial perspective on a subject that has already been exhaustively researched.

In the course of writing this book many people have been of great help. I would like to thank, particularly, H. Mark Roelofs for reading the manuscript in its many forms with a critical but always encouraging eye, and Dennis Anderson for his thoughtful and insightful comments. My thanks go also to John McGuigan, acquisitions editor at the University of Pennsylvania Press, for his confidence in the manuscript and his help in improving it; to my reviewers; to Peggy Hoover for her painstaking and thorough copyediting; and to Ingalill Hjelm, managing editor, for patiently guiding the manuscript to publication.

Last but not least, my thanks go to my husband, Ervin, for listening and advising, and to Isaac and Clara Shienbaum for their endless moral support.

ONE

WHO VOTES AND WHY: A CRITICAL LOOK AT THE CONSENSUS AND REVISIONIST VIEWS

The distinguishing feature and central argument of this book is that U.S. citizens exercise rationality not in choosing between political candidates but in deciding whether to vote at all. The evidence suggests that those able to benefit from (or at least live comfortably within) a political system in which tangible benefits are obtained for the most part outside the electoral process tend to make a rational choice to give the political system symbolic support by voting—and that those who are miserable and unable to use the system to better their state refrain from such a symbolic act, also rationally.

Readers familiar with the subject will undoubtedly find this proposition unorthodox, given conventional attempts to discover evidence of citizen rationality in the decision of who to vote for. Such attempts are based on the common view that voting not only ought to be, but is, an instrumental and purposive act, one through which citizens in a democracy make significant political choices by electing representatives who can later be held accountable. The assumption is that the choice between candidates in an election campaign will translate into public policy choices by the government brought into power by the election.

This general belief that voting is a crucial and instrumental act, a definiendum of democracy, and the subsequent pressure to vote reinforced through childhood socialization, is reflected in the tendency of many people to over-report the extent of their electoral participation. For example, in the 1976 presidential election survey conducted by the University of Michigan's Center for Political Studies, 71 percent of those asked "Did you vote in the election this fall?" answered affirmatively. Yet the actual vote count revealed that only 53 percent of the electorate cast their ballots, indicating that significant numbers of people felt considerable pressure to be less than totally candid concerning the extent of their electoral activity. There are only one or perhaps two other things that people are as unwilling to reveal publicly![1]

The general public is not alone in attaching such significance to voting. Public statements of politicians underscore their regard for the ballot. Lyndon Johnson, for example, in signing the Voting Rights Act of 1965, described the right to vote as "the most powerful instrument ever devised by man for breaking down injustice and destroying the terrible walls that imprison men because they are different from other men."[2] Political hyperbole notwithstanding, the presumption that voting is important because it confers tangible benefits is clearly reflected in the slogan adopted by the state of Pennsylvania to encourage voter registration: "It doesn't cost. It pays." Moreover, the image of the United States abroad as a democracy rests on the assumption that free and meaningful elections exist here. In fact, the United States has encouraged Third World nations to adopt the particular democratic procedure of elections, often as a condition for receiving aid.

Given the national commitment to elections, it is not surprising that the consensus view among U.S. political scientists is that voting is the most important participatory activity a citizen can undertake in the political system. Typical of many confident statements are these:

The vote merits attention because it is the most widely distributed of all political resources, because all decisions in a democratic form of government rest ultimately on votes and *it is the major mechanism* for translating popular preferences into governmental decisions.[3]

Voting is the most important and widespread political activity, and in terms of the impact of the citizenry on governmental performance it may be *the single* most important act.[4]

That umbrella of confidence extends also to the institution of elections, a leading defender of their role having once concluded that elections provided "only *one, but the most vital,* mandate."[5] Other more direct forms of participation between elections are acknowledged, but they have generally been regarded as of secondary importance, at least for the majority of citizens.

Who Votes and Why

Under the circumstances, it would be reasonable to expect not only that most citizens do vote but also that they do so responsibly, critically examining the candidates, carefully weighing the issues, and casting their votes accordingly.[6] On the contrary, however, large numbers of U.S. citizens (almost half in recent presidential elections) stay away from the polls, and there has been little conclusive evidence that those who do vote do so rationally. This is so despite the application of considerable methodological sophistication and technical virtuosity by political scientists bent on proving that the data suggest otherwise.[7]

How do we account for this disjunction between behavior and belief? One starting point would be to reexamine whether under current circumstances voting is in fact instrumentally meaningful, the chief way in which popular influence and control are exercised.

This task becomes even more pressing given the incontrovertible realities of the American political process. It hardly needs restating that American electoral politics operates under the twin handicaps of a fragmented institutional setting and weak political parties. In the latter instance, periodic urges to reform party operations have so weakened the parties that they are incapable of performing the functions conventionally associated with such organizations: recruiting and financing candidates, clarifying political issues, and acting as the vehicle for converting public choices into public policy.

Insofar as any of these things get done, candidates do them by and for themselves. At the presidential level particularly, the organizational weakness of parties has encouraged entrepreneurial candidacies, so much so that U.S. elections have become little more than publicly conducted, but essentially private battles to decide which individual will enjoy the fruits of elective office—the patronage, the power, and the prestige. Although we are concentrating on the national level, this is becoming true at all levels—state and local as well as national.

Consequently, we now have "personality politics." In and of itself, personality politics does not deny voters a meaningful, hence rational, choice, because they could always choose between the policies the candidates stood for individually. However, because the constitutional system of power is so fragmented, no one person can ever be held responsible for anything beyond his or her personal conduct in office, if that. The President, for instance, is constrained by so many shared responsibilities and so burdened with a constitutionally ordained congressional partnership that it becomes almost impossible for voters to assign responsibility for a given decision solely to the President. Hence voters cannot meaningfully apply checks or sanctions to the President's public conduct.

Moreover, given the reality of institutional fragmentation, it is apparent that the meaninglessness of electoral politics in the United States has roots deeper than the alleged decline of the party system. Therefore it is not a condition that can be easily corrected.

In any case, voters, faced with the severance of any consistent linkage between elections and public policy, and presented with electoral debates for the most part devoid of meaningful issue content, cannot be expected to make defensible choices between candidates or meaningful judgments on their past conduct. That this realization has reached the level of public awareness and debate is reflected in the following editorial comment in a leading newspaper on the congressional elections of 1982: "If the politicians do not pose the issues, the voters cannot decide them."[8] Given this state of affairs, it is plausible to suggest that those who do choose to vote anyway have made a rational decision to vote irrationally, because the political choices offered them by the system leave them only that alternative.

This hypothesis, however, raises still more questions. If voting is an act performed irrationally by those not expecting to gain tangible benefits by so doing, why is it performed at all? And by whom is it practiced? Moreover, what are the implications of an atrophied electoral process for the viability of American democracy?

Until now the only political scientists who have seriously questioned the instrumental significance of the electoral process, and in so doing provided some explanation of why people vote, have been the "revisionists"—those coming from the elitist or Marxist camps. Criticisms of elections similar to the criticisms we have mentioned, focusing on the lack of choices and of adequate checks, can be found in the work of C. Wright Mills, William Domhoff, and others. They concluded that the system is functionally undemocratic, conveying only the impression but not the reality of a political system designed to translate individual wants into satisfactory political outcomes.

Despite the electoral connection, the revisionists suggest that decision-making is in reality dominated by a closed elite variously described as the "military-industrial complex" or, by Marxists, as the "capitalist class." Thomas Dye, though not a proponent of this view, recently summed up the revisionist view:

Policy questions are seldom decided by the people through elections or through the presentation of policy alternatives by political parties. For the most part these "democratic" institutions—elections and parties—are important only for their symbolic value. They help tie the masses to the political system by giving them a role to play on election day and a political party with which they can identify.[9]

Dye's last point, that elections have symbolic rather than instrumental value, is especially important, because it hints at the revisionist explanation of who votes (i.e., "the masses") and why.

Since "the masses" are assumed to be excluded from meaningful participation, however, is it reasonable to conclude that, as in other electorally meaningless systems, elites are impervious to mass demands? While the revisionists are ambiguous on this point, it is implied that "the masses" receive disproportionately fewer benefits of the system. What role do elections play in such a system? They are, it has been suggested, events conducted by the few "haves" to provide the many "have-nots" with the illusion, though not the reality, of participation. Attracted by the ritualistic aspects of elections, the have-nots are reassured symbolically by the illusion of participation such events provide. It is a point of view that has been frequently and most cogently expressed by Murray Edelman: "Voting may be the most fundamental device for reassuring the masses that they are participants in the making of public policy."[10] Elections also provide a means of legitimating elite rule. Yet, overall, in the case of the United States, Michael Parenti concludes: "Elections . . . might better be considered a symbol of democratic governance than a guarantee of it, and voting often seems to be less an exercise than a surrender of sovereignty."[11] By implication, then, voters are irrational, even malleable, and participating in elections serves to promote their political quiescence and solidify their support for the political system (even if not for particular policies).

The most glaring problem with the revisionist explanation of who votes and why is that it is at odds with empirical reality. In the first place, the have-nots in the United States tend not to vote. Instead, it is the haves—those of middle-class status—who for the most part go to the polls. Moreover, in the American context (and by any fair accounting) the haves outnumber the have-nots, a reflection of the ability of the U.S. political and economic system to distribute benefits relatively broadly. (See Figure 1.)

While this book shares a common view of the role of elections in America with the revisionists—namely, that elections are primarily symbolic and expressive, rather than instrumental, events—it differs with them not only on the point argued above but also on a second point. The revisionists assume the political system to be essentially closed to the participation of all but a few, but this book is based on the premise that the fragmentation of

Beyond the Electoral Connection

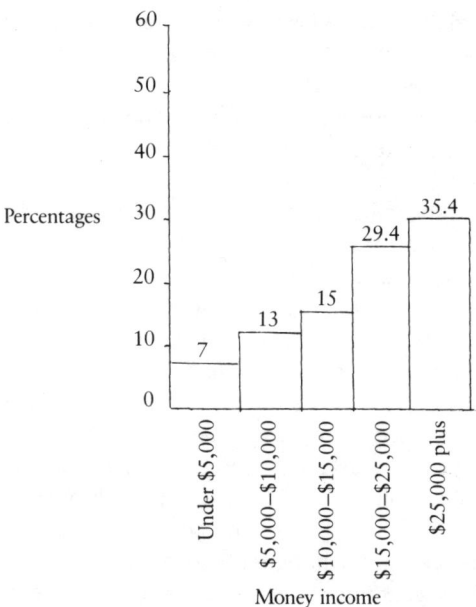

Figure 1

Money Income of Families in Constant U.S. Dollars, 1979

Source: Adapted from U.S. Bureau of the Census, *Statistical Abstract of the United States* (Washington, D.C., 1981), pp. 420, 425.

the American political system magnifies the opportunities for political participation. The system's pluralist and open character is emphasized by Morton Grodzins: "The normal process of policy making is one in which individuals and groups take their crack at influencing governmental policy at literally uncountable points in the legislative-administrative process."[12] As a result, the American political system is open to persons wishing to influence policy-making at many points other than elections.

Therefore, in contrast with the revisionist assumption that the United States is fundamentally undemocratic, this book will suggest that the system has retained its democratic features despite the breakdown of the electoral process. Nevertheless, it must be emphasized that the way the political process works has been substantially altered as a result of a combination of developmental circumstances, unique to the United States, that have served to open up alternative and more direct channels of instrumental political participation. These have grown in importance even as electoral linkages have become frayed.

From the very beginning, the United States responded differently from other democratic industrialized nations to the demands of the twentieth century, demands that everywhere produced an expansion of the public sector. As in Europe, the United States too experienced the pangs of economic and industrial growth, as well as the demands of wars and the dislocations they caused. Economic regulation of corporations came early on. Then the Depression, more than any other single event, led to a reluctant recognition that the government would have to play a larger and more continuing role in regulating the market cycle and in protecting those most likely to be hurt by them, such as farmers. This new awareness of the role of government was expanded by the demands of World War II for rapid mobilization. After the war, the urbanization and suburbanization of the United States called for an equally rapid expansion of government services, for example, sanitation and housing. Decades later, despite deregulation in some areas, such as commercial air travel and interstate trucking, government regulation in other areas such as health, safety, and the environment will not be easily curbed.

In other democratic industrialized nations, however, similar demands on the public sector for authoritative allocations of resources were met almost solely by a growth of legislative-executive activity and importance—that is, by an increase in the decisions made by the elected organs of government. Those decisions were, as in Great Britain, for instance, based on programs of action presented to and chosen by voters at elections and enacted by strong, responsible parties.

In the United States, however, a similar development was initially inhibited by a political ideology—laissez-faire liberalism—that proscribed government action, and by a fragmented institutional setting that encouraged legislative-executive deadlock. Moreover, over the past twenty years, that deadlock of decision-making, which has prevented a coherent public policy response to critical problems, has been reinforced if not exacerbated by weakened party organizations. Consequently, the public policy disgorged by the elected branches is ad hoc, piecemeal, incrementally accumulated, and, most crucially, unrelated to elections. Even more important, however, such decision-making powers are broadly shared with two other institutions that have been brought into the public policy process participating alongside the elected branches: the courts and the bureaucracy.

The bureaucracy has not only grown in size and importance but has done so by means of a unique creation, the independent regulatory commission, expressly designed in order to be free of political (hence electoral) control and given practically free rein to make rules in conformance with its own standards. In addition, as Theodore Lowi has argued in *The End of Liberalism,* the power to make allocative decisions has been recently expanded by congressional delegations of power to the bureaucracy through vague legislative mandates that require administrators to set standards. In doing so, they make public policy de facto. Then, it is argued, when conflicts occur either because administrative units with overlapping jurisdictions but competing interests disagree, or because administrative units and their affected clientele conflict, the courts are prevailed on to interpret congressional intent. For example, in a recent case concerning workers' exposure to cotton dust, the U.S. Supreme Court in 1981 ruled against the use of cost-benefit analysis by the Occupational Safety and Health Administration which had been directed by the Office of Management and Budget to use this method to reduce regulatory expenses for industry. In arriving at this ruling, the Court interpreted the congressional mandate to OSHA and recommended instead that the agency use a cost-effective approach to worker safety and health, balancing the costs and benefits of a particular regulation against alternative regulations designed to reach the same level of protection.[13]

To be sure, the courts in the United States have always played a unique role in comparison with those of Europe. Ever since Chief Justice John Marshall seized the initiative of judicial review of congressional actions, legislative supremacy has been in doubt. Lately those doubts have been enlarged as the courts have embarked on occasionally massive reinterpretations of legislative will by means of statutory reinterpretation.

The reason both bodies have assumed an activist stance with respect to the making of authoritative decisions for U.S. society is that the elected branches are all too frequently unwilling or unable to resolve divisive political questions on their own. Because of increasing demands on the political system, and the inadequate response of the elected branches, judges today are no longer impartial adjudicators of legislative will, nor are bureaucrats merely conduits of legislative purpose. The shift in decision-making gravity to de facto decision-makers outside the electoral process has seen a concomitant shift in the focus of public participation and interest. In part, that increase in extra-electoral participatory activity was mandated by Congress, beginning with the Administrative Procedures Act of 1946 and increasing throughout the 1960s and 1970s. In part, it has occurred because the judiciary has been increasingly receptive to the inclusion of parties claiming noneconomic injuries in judicial proceedings from which they had been formerly excluded. The recent past has consequently seen extensive revisions in rules of legal standing, sovereign immunity, and due process. And attempts in the 1980s to roll back this process have not been very successful—a point to be substantiated as the discussion proceeds.

As a result of these alterations of the political process, public participation in policy-making is able to proceed by means of a selection of extra-electoral channels, all of them relatively permeable. If one channel appears likely to be unresponsive or blocked, an alternative is available. For example, the battle for black civil rights between the *Plessy* and *Brown* decisions (in fact, until the Voting Rights Act of 1965) was fought not through the legislature but almost exclusively through the courts. This generalization is confirmed by a study of blacks in Durham, North Carolina, by William Keech, who concluded that "the really striking gains of Durham's Negro minority have come through resources other than votes."[14]

Thus, even as elections have become less and less meaningful and their impact on policy decisions more difficult to discern, additional extra-electoral channels of influence (judicial and bureaucratic) have taken their place, creating a system in which tangible benefits are increasingly obtained outside the electoral process. Even as electoral linkages recede in importance, the democratic character of the system has been retained through an expansion of direct opportunities to influence public policy. Through intervention in administrative proceedings or through court orders, interest groups, both public and private, can force the government into specific actions on their behalf.[15]

The operative realities of American politics which we have just described are considerably more complex than they would be if the United States conformed to its ideal of an electoral democracy. In an electoral democracy, people perform a relatively simple act—voting—and by doing so choose representatives who will make public policy in accordance with the mandates of that election.

In the United States, however, public policy is created and defined not during but after an election is over, by an ongoing process that is open to public input. But because it is a more complex system, it requires that participants have a relatively high degree of political sophistication and technical competence. The resources required for effective participation are therefore more substantial than those required for voting, so that not everyone will be able to engage in extra-electoral participation, or can do so successfully.

Nevertheless, those resources are not so substantial that, as many critics believe, they are possessed only by the privileged few.[16] Technical expertise, money, and political experience can all be acquired by those citizens who comprise the broad mass of middle-class Americans who tend to be white, well educated, and relatively affluent. They possess, or can acquire, the requisite skills to engage in direct contacting forms of participation which are more costly in terms of time and effort, if not money, than voting. For instance, the middle classes are more likely to be members of organized interest groups that will press their professional demands on relevant bureaucrats, or as consumers to join the growing number of public interest pressure groups. They are also more likely, when thwarted by the elected branches or by the bureaucracy, to circumvent their authority by appeals to the judicial process.

In any case, these people—the haves—will be more likely to see their lives filled with opportunities for advancement and advantage. *It is from these ranks that voters in America are drawn.* Not all those who benefit vote, but enough do vote that every study of voters indicates that voting levels increase with rising socioeconomic status.

Such people are certainly educated and intelligent enough to discern the noninstrumental, hence symbolic, character of voting, but they are prepared to go to the polls nonetheless. Why? Partly it is a consequence of habit reinforced since childhood by political socialization. More important, however (and it is this that explains the class bias of voting more than anything else), they probably vote as a gesture of support for a political system within which they have been able to live comfortably. Hence, it is logical to assume that for them voting is first and foremost an act of social responsibility requiring their presence in the voting booth. And because it *is* recognized as an act of civic duty, it tends to be performed with minimal ratiocination. Jack Dennis hinted at this possibility some time ago when he found that "educational attainment improves one's sense of voting duty and approval of the way the system operates . . . but it decreases the [belief] that elections are effective."[17]

The fact that beneficiaries of the system are more prone to engage in a symbolic act should not in and of itself be surprising. In any social structure, it is the "haves" who tend to be supporters of certain conventions and mores that reinforce the status quo, especially those with a strong normative component. From that standpoint, belief in voting is little different from belief in marriage. Both tend to be practiced by the middle classes in terms of principle, while frequently supplemented, if not circumvented, by other activities in practice.

11
Who Votes and Why

On the other hand, there exist several strata in American society who define themselves as largely outside the system. Without political sophistication, technical expertise, or material resources, its members are unable to take advantage of these complex channels of influence. On the periphery of American society and less advantageously situated, they have less access and fewer assets with which to press their demands. They are the poor, sometimes the young and frequently those of minority status—those on the periphery of American society. Their position renders them less able to press their demands through extra-electoral channels. Lobbying and litigation (civil rights legislation notwithstanding) are usually beyond the capacities of these groups. Having little reason to engage in what amounts to an act of legitimation, the have-nots have responded to the electoral process, as they have to other societal rituals, by ignoring it.

The argument should not be stretched too thin. Not all have-nots abstain. Some do vote. Possibly those who are aspiring haves or who subjectively define themselves as such will be more likely to go to the polls. Conversely, not all the haves vote, but more of them do than do not.

Hence, while agreeing with the revisionists that U.S. elections are largely symbolic events, on the basis of our presumption that the system is procedurally democratic we differ on why people vote. Voters are not the mass of have-nots duped into political quiescence by the illusion of participation and the promise of tangible benefits never received. Rather, voters are the *haves*—the beneficiaries of the system who rationally choose to vote as an expression of their support for the system. Since these people constitute a plurality of citizens not only by income but also by temperament and inclination, we can surmise that their support is sufficiently broad-based to ensure the stability of the system, at least for the present.

Our general argument obviously has implications for the direction of public policy with respect to nonvoting. Its extent, compared with other democracies, is disquieting. But if we are correct, and voting is something Americans do only *after* they have received tangible benefits, and not something they do *in order* to obtain them (as democratic theory suggests), it stands to reason that certain currently proposed remedies for boosting the rate of voting which focus on procedural alterations of elections themselves (e.g., the elimination of registration requirements) will not have the intended effect.

What we must do to encourage the more widespread practice of voting is first enable the have-nots to compete more effectively in a political system in which tangible benefits are paradoxically obtained outside electoral channels. Assuming that these channels of participation are open and that such groups have been excluded from effective participation by reason of political incompetence, political inexperience, or political deprivation, educational programs to eliminate these handicaps should prove a useful initial step. The ill-fated community action programs of the 1960s did attempt to help the poor bargain for resources outside the standard electoral setting, but since these programs did nothing to help the poor become more qualified to compete through extra-electoral channels, they failed in their purpose. The idea of including neighborhood groups in the decision-making process resurfaced in 1978 in President Jimmy Carter's now moribund urban policy speech. But it is an idea worth reviving if adequate preparation and training is to be provided such groups. Otherwise we can expect these groups to continue to engage increasingly in sporadic and anomic modes of communication, such as riots and acts of vandalism. In any case, until the have-nots receive tangible benefits from the system, they cannot be expected to express their support for it by voting.

The book is organized as follows: Chapter 2 explores in more detail our view of the electoral process as essentially noninstrumental, marked as it is by organizationally frail political parties operating in a system of institutional fragmentation. We will review the extensive literature on voting behavior and reexamine it to show that the "haves" have adjusted to these realities by making rational choices to go to the polls but then casting their votes with minimal ratiocination (i.e., irrationally).

Chapter 3 will emphasize the pluralist character of the political process. It will note that Congress and to a lesser extent the President, though important in setting forth broad policy goals, make policy quite independently of being elected, and that they are joined in policy-making by the courts and bureaucracy, both of which have been playing a greatly expanded role in recent years. It will also present the findings of more recent studies of participation which indicate that citizen input is increasingly directed through these channels and that such participation is markedly rational and instrumental.

Chapter 4 will present the findings of several empirical studies in support of my hypothesis: (1) It is the beneficiaries of the system who vote. (2) They have chosen to do so noninstrumentally, viewing it as an expression of civic duty by which to make their own lives, political gains, and egos meaningful.

In the last chapter, we will confront the issue of whether a system in which elections have only a vestigial instrumental role can be called a democracy at all. Clearly the United States is not a democracy in the conventional sense—that is to say, it is not a representative/electoral democracy.

Who Votes and Why

Since Joseph Schumpeter, modern conceptions of democracy have tended to be based on the British model, which emphasizes both elections and a dominant role for responsible parties. In that model, however, public participation is actually limited to voting by means of which citizens choose between alternative competing groups and control their actions by voting them out of office. The actual choice of who can run in an election and on what platform is entirely the domain of organized and responsible parties.

In fact, American (nonacademic) conceptions of democracy have always differed considerably from the British model that Schumpeter so admired. First, the American popular ideal of democracy stressed citizen participation in all phases of politics. To the extent that popular participation during elections in what were formerly party activities has now been achieved, the conditions for an electoral democracy have all but disappeared. In addition, the very multiplicity of elective offices and the consequent fragmentation of the political process (which makes programmatic politics impossible) paradoxically makes the system susceptible to penetration outside and between elections. Moreover, as Austin Ranney reminded us, underlying this urge for achieving maximum popular participation has been a strong drive to avoid one of the things an electoral democracy inevitably produces—majority rule. Indeed, the American political system, with its opportunities for filibustering and the like, was carefully constructed to avoid and prevent majority rule from ever occurring.[18]

Despite these realities, the dialogue between the consensus and revisionist schools has continued as if the United States were an electoral democracy. Now, however, those in the consensus camp who proclaim the United States to be democratic find themselves hard-pressed to frame their case in terms of meaningful elections. Perhaps that is because only in the context of a legitimizing myth is the United States a representative democracy. In its day-to-day operations, the system by and large functions independently of elections. However, the revisionists who malign the United States as undemocratic because its elections *are* meaningless either ignore alternative channels of political participation or assume them to be used only by the few.

We shall therefore suggest that an alternative definition of democracy be adopted, one that does not rely on elections as a primary and requisite feature. The term "citizen participant democracy" appears to best fit the type of political system in which mass participation is continuous, not minimally confined to voting, procedurally open, and highly susceptible to nonelectoral penetration. It is through these means that popular influence over policy is secured. Moreover control over policymakers, an essential element of a democracy, also exists, not to any meaningful extent through electoral sanctions but through the institutional checks and balances built into the American political system. As a citizen-participant democracy, the United States is certainly unique among other democracies, where voting is the first and foremost step in the political process.

In the United States, however, contrary to conventional wisdom, voting is not the most important participatory act in the political process and is very likely recognized for what it is—an act of retroactive legitimation—by those citizens who benefit from the status quo and who therefore are more likely to choose to go to the polls. The chapter will conclude by reassessing the significance of elections and their present role in the political process. The argument will be made that even though elections are for the most part legitimating events, they do make an important contribution to the stability of the political system.

Notes

1. It has been suggested that this is due to a "panel activation" effect, which occurs in before-and-after surveys. Yet overreporting of the voting act also appears in after-only election surveys, such as those conducted by the Census Bureau, as well as in the New Jersey survey conducted by this author in 1981.
2. Lyndon Johnson, quoted in *Newsweek*, August 16, 1965, p. 15.
3. William Keech, *The Impact of Negro Voting: The Role of the Vote in the Quest for Equality* (Chicago: Rand McNally & Co., 1968), p. 3. Emphasis added.
4. Sidney Verba and Norman Nie, *Participation in America: Democracy and Social Equality* (New York: Harper & Row, 1972), p. 46. Emphasis added.
5. Gerald Pomper, *Elections in America: Control and Influence in American Politics* (New York: Dodd, Mead & Co. 1968), p. 266. Emphasis added.
6. These conditions for voter rationality were originally set by Angus Campbell et al., *The American Voter* (New York: John Wiley & Sons, 1960).
7. This point will be substantiated at greater length in Chapter 2.
8. *Wall Street Journal*, November 2, 1982, p. 28.
9. Thomas Dye, *Understanding Public Policy*, 3d ed. (Englewood Cliffs, N.J.: Prentice-Hall, 1972), p. 301.
10. Murray Edelman, *The Symbolic Uses of Politics* (Urbana: University of Illinois Press, 1964), p. 189.

11. Michael Parenti, *Democracy for the Few* (New York: St. Martin's Press, 1974), p. 165.
12. Morton Grodzins in *The American System*, ed. Daniel Elazar (Chicago: Rand McNally & Co., 1966), p. 6.
13. *Wall Street Journal*, July 7, 1981, p. 1.
14. Keech, *Impact of Negro Voting*, p. 15.
15. For an extended discussion of this point, see Joseph Califano, *Governing America: An Insider's Report from the White House and Cabinet* (New York: Simon & Schuster, 1981).
16. Morris Fiorina (*Retrospective Voting in American Elections* [New Haven: Yale University Press, 1981]) has summarized critics' objections to the pluralist argument: "Perhaps such accounts rang true for the 'masses' composed of oilmen, doctors, and government workers, but what of the masses of the aged, the poor, and consumers?" (p. 4). We are arguing here that the "mass" of U.S. citizens are largely middle class and that they, as consumers, for example, have in recent years organized themselves to obtain representation of their interests through extraelectoral channels. This point is argued in greater detail in Chapter 3.
17. Jack Dennis, "Support for the Institution of Elections by the Mass Public," *American Political Science Review* 74 (September 1970): 833.
18. Austin Ranney, "Towards a More Responsible Two-party System: A Commentary," *American Political Science Review* 45 (June 1951): 488-99. An intriguing alternate view is Martin Diamond, "Democracy and the Federalist: A Reconsideration of the Framers' Intent," *American Political Science Review* 53 (March 1959): 52-68. In opposition to the view that the Constitution avoided majority rule, Diamond states that in the amending procedure, for example, the "real aim and practical effect . . . was not at all to give power to minorities, but to ensure that passage of an amendment would require a *nationally* distributed majority, though one that legally could consist of a numerical majority." Though his presentation is interesting, Diamond does not address all the other devices (e.g., the filibuster) that do serve to prevent even national majorities from forming easily.

TWO

VOTING AS AN ACT OF POLITICAL RITUALISM

The heated and seemingly endless debates over whether citizens behave rationally (instrumentally) have focused primarily on people's behavior inside the polling booth. In other words, debate has focused on the decision of who to vote for rather than on the rationality of the decision whether to go to the polls at all. The former emphasis can be easily explained. Elections are assumed to be at the core of the American political process, and it follows that, through their choices between candidates, citizens can secure political influence over the direction of future government policy and retain control over decision-makers.

Based on the assumption that voting is essentially a choice between candidates based on expectations of their *future* performance (prospective voting), Gerald Pomper states: "Voters can meaningfully intervene to support a leadership group which is seeking to enact a particular program. By their endorsements of particular contestants in the bargaining process the voters can have the final word. *The choice of governors can thereby become a choice of government policy.*"[1] Other and more recent efforts have chosen to focus on retrospective voting, that is, voting as a judgment on *past* performance. Morris Fiorina, for instance, suggests, "elections do not signal the direction in which society should move so much as they convey an evaluation of where society has been."[2] Pomper claims, "To exert their influence, voters have the most obvious and vital sanction: they control the politician's job. They can quickly and bloodlessly dismiss an offensive official and thereby end his power, prestige and profit."[3]

Although voters in a democracy are supposed to have control over politicians and influence over their policies through the ballot, American practice is demonstrably at odds with democratic theory woven into electoral myth. These descriptive and prescriptive evaluations of the role of voting have not been definitively confirmed by empirical investigations of voting behavior. When deciding among political candidates, citizens are quite likely to ignore the issues, perhaps even abandon the party for which they are registered and decide on the basis of a candidate's "image," switching votes and splitting tickets with promiscuous abandon. It seems to be the case that their political convictions are labile and their electoral behavior volatile. And once having made a choice, the average citizen tends to reelect incumbents, often even corrupt ones, eschewing the opportunity to hold public officials accountable for their actions. In sum, the average citizen does not behave the way democratic citizens are supposed to behave, that is, with a rational concern for the quality of candidates and a discriminating interest in policy choices. Even the most recent studies have done little to erase the unflattering image of the voter portrayed by the earliest investigators—such as Bernard Berelson and Angus Campbell and their colleagues—a point to be substantiated as the discussion proceeds.

The goal of this chapter is to explain why instrumental considerations play such a small part in arriving at the voting decision. At the crux of this argument is the proposition that "incompetent" and "irresponsible" voting represents a tacit recognition on the part of an increasingly sophisticated electorate that the conditions under which prospective, or even retrospective, voting might meaningfully occur are to a large extent absent. To imply, however, that the ignorant voter may not after all be irrational is not in and of itself an original proposition. Rational-choice theorists, using simplified analytical models derived from mathematics and economics, arrived at similar conclusions some years back. Anthony Downs, for example, assumed a desire for rational human beings to maximize their utilities and suggested rational calculations on the part of voters that the costs of acquiring information simply exceeded the benefits to be gained from voting.[4]

The conclusions of the Downsian model, as well as those of others, were arrived at on logical grounds, not on empirical grounds. Taking account of the operative realities of American politics in this analysis, it is to be suggested that the benefits of voting—namely, influence and control—cannot be obtained in the absence of functional political parties. The deterioration of political parties, superimposed on a fragmented institutional structure, has, we shall argue, effectively transformed elections into expensive sideshows that only marginally affect political outcomes. In particular, parties have been left with minimal control over the recruitment of political candidates, who are now able to seek funding from a variety of public and private sources outside the party organization. Consequently, the party is unable to influence the quality and direction of public debate during elections, or to demand that public officials toe the party line afterward. In the absence of programmatic elections and without the imposition of legislative discipline, no candidate can personally fulfill his or her campaign promises or be held accountable if he or she does not. Hence voters are effectively denied a rational basis for choosing one candidate over another, so they have tended to shift the direction of rational participatory activity toward extra-electoral channels and away from an electoral process captured by politically "irresponsible" entrepreneurs. (See Chapter 3.) In this chapter we will document the nature of voters' apparently irrational response to the electoral process from the perspective that it constitutes a rational adjustment to current political realities, and explain why it has occurred, concentrating on presidential elections, where party decomposition has been the most severe.

Voter Adjustments to the Electoral Process

The behavior of voters seems to indicate that they recognize only too clearly the receding role of political parties and the increasingly noninstrumental nature of elections. From this perspective, two central facts about voting behavior which tend to be considered "irrational" become perfectly understandable: (1) Voters tend to ignore both party labels and issues in their choice of leaders, voting instead on the basis of "image." (2) Voters tend to reelect incumbents, rejecting the opportunity to hold elected officials accountable. Each of these tendencies will be examined and analyzed separately.

Do Voters Make Prospective Choices?

Several empirical studies (beginning with the landmark study of U.S. voters in 1954 by Berelson, Lazarfeld, and McPhee[5] and spanning over two decades) confirm the noninstrumental basis on which voters make their political choices. Assessing the evidence of the 1960s, Michael Shapiro has written: "If any one unifying conception has emerged from the original large scale studies it is that the voter is irrational."[6] In the 1970s, Michael Margolis, another critical observer, came to essentially the same conclusion. He notes that "issues have continued to play only a relatively minor role as determinants of voting choice in Presidential elections."[7] And even dissenters of the view that voters make uninformed choices, notably Gerald Pomper and David RePass, have nevertheless found candidate image to be the most important factor in the voting decision. For instance, in a recent study of the 1972 election, Pomper and Mark Schulman found that the candidate variable (.366) outweighed the issue variable (.233),[8] which is in keeping with the findings of David RePass for the 1964 presidential election.[9] Even the correlations for the 1976 election seem to underscore this. As Arthur Miller and his associates admit, "Candidate ratings in 1976, as in previous elections, were strongly related with vote choice at the individual level. Moreover, issue consistency was low."[10] They go on to say that "economic attitudes clearly had an impact on the electoral outcome but that impact was reduced by several factors, including the tendency of individuals to cast their ballots in a manner inconsistent with their economic evaluations and their economic self-interest."[11]

If these conclusions about the behavior of voters had been generally accepted within the profession, however, the debate over whether voters qua voters behave irrationally would have ended long ago. But the "incompetent voter" runs contrary to electoral myth, which required citizens to behave rationally at the polls. Most recently there has been an attempt to resurrect the textbook version of the rational citizen as one who recognizes issues, correctly identifies candidates' positions on the issues, and then makes an informed decision inside the polling booth. The debate rages on, given impetus initially by V. O. Key's posthumously published book *The Responsible Electorate*,[12] in which Key claimed to have found evidence of voter rationality. Lately the debate has been fueled by the findings of equally respected scholars, such as the team led by Sidney Verba and Norman Nie, and by Gerald Pomper, who has for some time toiled hard to unearth definitive evidence that voters behave rationally at the polls.

Claiming to have used more sophisticated methodological techniques and a more comprehensive data base than in his previous efforts, Pomper, in partnership with Mark Schulman, claims to have discovered a rise in the salience of issues and increasing perceptions by voters of differences between the parties. On the first point, the authors confidently report, "While new voters in 1964 and 1972 demonstrate greater issue responsiveness than the older 1956 cohorts they presumably replaced, a substantial increase in issue voting is evident across time in all generational cohorts."[13]

Pomper's findings on the importance of issues are similar to those of Norman Nie, Sidney Verba, and John Petrocik in *The Changing American Voter,* a work remarkably broad in scope. The authors enthusiastically conclude, "We can find independent evidence for an increase in issue *importance* that comes at the same time as the sharp step upward in issue *consistency.*"[14] We remain skeptical of the results of this scholarship. Given the present electoral context, the findings seem unlikely.

There have recently emerged a bevy of younger political scientists, trained in statistics and well versed in computer skills, who are prepared to do battle with the findings of these senior scholars precisely on the methodological grounds on which their studies rest. The most trenchant and thorough of such attacks has been mounted by Michael Margolis. Writing in the *American Political Science Review,* he acknowledges the utility of sophisticated techniques: "No one can seriously gainsay the advantages of new and powerful statistical techniques. We know they offer subtle insights which cruder old-fashioned analyses failed to uncover." Then he goes on to admonish, "Yet in applying them to issue voting, political scientists must proceed with caution, taking care that a fascination with discovering relationships between issues and voting among subgroups of the population does not overwhelm an appreciation of these subgroups in comparison with others in the general population."[15]

Applying this very standard to an influential and controversial 1972 article by Pomper entitled "From Confusion to Clarity: Issues and the American Voter," Margolis proceeds to dismantle Pomper's findings one by one. To begin with, he challenges one of Pomper's main findings, which purports to show an increase in voters who satisfy the prerequisite of having an opinion and who perceive differences in party positions on five issues. He is particularly critical of the fact that Pomper does not reveal the total sample size on which his conclusions are based, making it impossible to tell the extent to which those voters included in the tables were typical of the general population.

Suspicious of statistical chicanery, Margolis returned to the original data compiled by the Survey Research Center at the University of Michigan and recomputed it, basing his percentages on the *N*s for the entire sample rather than only on those *N*s perceiving differences between the parties. This change in methodology yields a conclusion that is less clear-cut than the one reached by Pomper: "Far from showing that in the 1960s the great bulk of the population came to perceive party differences, or for that matter that they came to agree upon these preferences, the table shows more modest increases in awareness of and polarization on the issues."[16]

Nor does Pomper's data even indicate a trend toward greater issue awareness, as he claimed. In fact, on one issue—that of school integration—the 1972 data revealed that only 34 percent of the population had any possibility of voting on the basis of this issue, exactly the same percentage as in 1956.

Margolis goes on to fire another salvo. He contends that certain findings were more a result of the techniques and modes of analysis used than a true reflection of actual relationships in the data, thereby casting considerable suspicion on any conclusions that imply voter rationality.

He even picks out embarrassingly simple statistical flaws; for example, in Arthur Miller's study of the 1972 presidential contest between Richard Nixon and George McGovern, Miller and his colleagues purported to have discovered the emergence of greater issue-consciousness on the part of voters. The authors had claimed that in this election the distribution of votes was associated with the issue positions of the voters regardless of the voters' partisan identifications. Margolis is critical of Miller's methodology on two counts. First, he argues that Boyd's "normal vote analysis," a technique which Miller borrowed and on which his findings were based, has a number of conceptual flaws. By aggregating the responses of respondents, it reduces the variance to be explained, thereby producing an artificially high linear correlation. Margolis experimented with the data himself and found that on the Vietnam issue, for example, a 9 variable rather than a 7 variable multiple regression analysis (such as that used by Miller et al.) would not have yielded as high a correlation, casting doubt on Miller's contention that a significant relationship between a voter's position on the issues and his or her choice of a candidate had been discovered. Second, Margolis questions the validity of the entire multiple regression analysis on the basis that there is so much multi-colinearity in the variables used that no valid conclusions can be drawn.

Other methodological attacks question the format of the surveys themselves. This charge has been leveled at the 1976 findings of Nie, Verba, and Petrocik in their widely acclaimed *The Changing American Voter*, which purported to show that the breakdown of partisanship led to the emergence of ideological thinking and the growth of issue voting. The criticisms of two studies in particular suggest that extreme caution should be exercised before relying on the interpretations of that study with respect to issue salience.

George Bishop and his colleagues have subjected the questionnaires themselves to rigorous scrutiny. They concluded, "There has been little or no change since the non-ideological 1950s" and attribute much of the apparent shift in mass sophistication to what they term a "basic methodological artifact," changes in question wording and format. Moreover, they not only extend this critique to the work of Norman Nie and his associates, but also maintain, "Our findings apply just as well to the equally acclaimed work by Gerald Pomper and others on issue voting."[17] Working independently to reexamine the same surveys, a similar conclusion was reached by John Sullivan and his colleagues, who likewise concluded, "Constraint in the mass public probably did not increase very much between 1950 and 1976. Rather, reported changes were due to modifications in the survey items used to measure constraint."[18]

To the extent that issue voting has been found to occur at all, Edward Carmines and James Stimson suggest that it occurs mostly on "easy issues," which they describe as "symbolic rather than technical," "more likely to deal with policy ends than with means," and "items long on the political agenda." It is crucial that they found that easy-issue voting was concentrated in the *least* sophisticated portion of the electorate.[19]

We must reemphasize that voters are capable of discerning issues and of behaving rationally even during elections. On those rare occasions when voters are presented with issues in the form of referenda, voters show a remarkable facility for voting rationally (on the basis of the issues) and "correctly" (in keeping with their preferences) even when the referendum wording seems to obfuscate the issue. An unusual study by Dennis Anderson of a recent referendum in Ohio on the issue of election day registration is a case in point.[20] The referendum in question involved a proposed amendment to the Ohio constitution to repeal the state's recently enacted (1977) election day registration law, dubbed the "instant voter law," and to reimpose the closing date for registering of thirty days before the election. Voters therefore were not asked to vote directly on whether or not they wanted election day registration but on whether they were for or against the repeal of the new registration law. On the referendum itself, a vote against election day registration required a *yes* vote (i.e., a vote for repeal of the amendment), and a vote for the election day registration required a *no* vote (i.e., a vote against repeal of the amendment).

This was a confusing situation, yet the rate of mis-voting was rather small. Only 15 percent of the sample were estimated to have mis-voted, indicating that voters are capable, under certain circumstances, of making the transition from expressive to instrumental voting, whereas under "normal" circumstances (voting for candidates) they revert to "image" voting.

Such "irrational" behavior constitutes a rational adjustment to an electoral process that only to a vestigial extent provides organizational links between citizens and their government. In theory, those linkages were to be provided by operational political parties that structured choices among political candidates and disciplined their activities in office. The deterioration of American political parties to the point where they are for all practical purposes nonfunctional is, as we shall presently show, recognized by those who choose to go to the polls. Academic accounts of the parties' decline are numerous, and a brief review of them follows.

The Disintegration of Parties in the Electoral Process

American political parties were not always as organizationally incoherent and inconsequential as they are now. They were once well organized, professionally led, and dominated by party regulars. In fact, several observers have implied that political parties once played a major role in producing nonincremental changes in policy following such periodic crises as wars or depressions. These crises, it is said, served to precipitate electoral realignments during which voters expressed their dissatisfaction with the candidates and the policy of the party in power by suddenly and swiftly shifting their allegiances en masse to the opposition party. During such "critical" elections, new issues emerged and became part of a fresh political agenda. On the basis of this, the new majority party was able to push through major changes in the direction of public policy.

Walter Dean Burnham, who has written extensively on the subject, has identified the elections of 1800, 1828, 1860, 1896, and 1932 as "critical" and maintains: "They are intimately associated with and followed by transformations in large clusters of policy. This produces correspondingly profound alterations in policy and influences the grand institutional structures of American government."[21] Similarly Barbara Sinclair, assessing the policy changes that occurred after the last "critical" election, that of 1932, is impressed by the broad scope of postelection transformations of public policy. She too has asserted: "The emergence of social welfare legislation as a regular element of the political agenda is directly traceable to the great depression and the realignment it precipitated. The most clearly non-incremental social welfare programs were passed during the height of the realigning era and little non-incremental legislation ever came close to passing during the remainder of the period under study."[22]

These and other studies appear to suggest that at one time U.S. elections did provide citizens with meaningful choices (i.e., choices that resulted in programmatic change) and an opportunity to "vote the rascals out"—in other words, with "influence" over policy and "control" over politicians. Moreover, the high levels of voter turnout and partisan identification recorded suggest that voters in turn were able to respond to a political context in which electorally generated change was possible. This is no longer the case. Few observers are currently prepared to argue that political parties are strong enough to capture the attention or the loyalty of citizens dissatisfied with their own party, or to generate programmatic change.

It is generally acknowledged that, since 1932 and despite recurrent crises, no new major electoral realignments have occurred. Whereas realignments were once triggered by crises that caused voters to abandon one party and climb aboard another, over the past forty years (in fact, since 1932) parties have ceased to be effective vehicles for generating and organizing political controversy. Consequently Burnham, noting that parties are now incapable of articulating and organizing political change, fears that they may eventually disappear altogether.[23] And E. E. Schattschneider's prescient description of political parties as organizationally "incoherent" more than forty years ago reflects the current consensus of informed opinion on the subject.[24]

There are several reasons for the current weakened state of American political parties. Part of the problem can be attributed to the periodic urges to democratize and reform party operations. Earlier attempts by the Progressives had introduced the unique device of the "primary." By wresting control of the party nomination from the "bosses" and tossing it into the popular arena, this one reform was a major factor in diluting party control over its own label. This reformist bent, however, resurfaced with even greater force during the 1970s. The extent and scope of these reforms is reflected in Austin Ranney's claim that "taken together . . . the two national parties have made more reforms from 1968 to 1975 than at any time since the death of the congressional caucus and the birth of the national conventions in the 1820s and 1830s."[25] Hence even Pomper, who had once confidently written that "the two-party system is the most important fact about American elections," is now prepared to acknowledge that "the state of the party appears rather pitiful when sketched at the present time."[26] As a result of this reformist bent, Pomper notes that parties have lost control over two vital elements—recruitment and resources—which had ensured their electoral primacy in the past.

A major reason for the recent rapid decline of party control over presidential recruitment has been the increase in the number of presidential nominating primaries, thirty-five in 1980, and the Democratic changes in the rules regarding delegate selection following the report of the McGovern-Frazer Commission. In most states that now have primaries, delegates are assigned to presidential candidates on the basis of the proportion of the popular vote they win. Those delegates are bound to vote for the candidate they represent at least on the first ballot, and they are entitled to replace any delegate whose support seems equivocal with more loyal substitutes. Since the choices of delegates to a large extent are now determined by the popular vote, and since they are pledged in advance to particular candidates, the national nominating conventions have become essentially pro forma events, especially for the Democrats, the new procedures having lessened the powers of state and local leaders as power brokers.

These changed circumstances are exemplified by a comparison of the political campaigns of John Kennedy in 1960 and the campaign of his brother Edward in 1980. John Kennedy campaigned in far fewer primaries than his brother did twenty years later, and he did so with the knowledge that they were essentially "beauty contests," which in no way diminished his obligation to mend fences with the traditional party organization. By 1980, however, the influence of party leaders was so vitiated that Edward Kennedy was able to consider seriously, and then mount, a challenge against an incumbent President of his own party and even win several primaries in states where he was pointedly not endorsed by the local party leadership. In New Jersey, for example, a popular local congressman, James Florio, endorsed Jimmy Carter, Kennedy obtaining only the support of Mayor Angelo Errichetti of Camden, a man tainted by the Abscam bribery scandal. Kennedy nevertheless won the New Jersey primary. By the same token, even though Chicago Mayor Jane Byrne endorsed him, she was unable to deliver the state's vote to Kennedy as her seasoned predecessor Richard Daley had once been able to do for his brother.

The weakened hold of the party organization over the recruitment of political candidates has effectively opened up the nominating process to political outsiders who stand a reasonable chance of becoming the party nominee with a personal political organization forged over a year or two. A prime illustration was the phenomenon of Jimmy Carter, virtually unknown to the public in 1975 but able to secure his party's nomination barely one year later.

Perhaps more critical, party dominance over campaign funds has been eroded, in part as a result of post-Watergate reforms in 1974 and 1976. In presidential elections, public money in the form of matching grants is given *directly* to candidates rather than through the party organizations. President Jimmy Carter's State of the Union Message in 1979 urged that public funding be extended to congressional candidates as well, and if this reform is ever enacted it will effectively deal a deathblow to the already tottering state party organizations. Even so, in House and Senate elections, private money is being given directly to candidates through the newly formed political action committees and is not being funneled through party organizations. In any case, the amount of aid given by national party organizations to senatorial and congressional candidates was always minimal and mattered most to marginal candidates unable to obtain it elsewhere.

In a legislative effort to preserve and extend the democratic spirit implied in party reform, Congress had in 1974 enacted spending limitations for those presidential candidates accepting public funds. However, the entrepreneurial candidacies of the personally wealthy have been boosted by a recent U.S. Supreme Court ruling which stated that individual candidates are not limited by how much of their own money they can spend (*Buckley v. Valeo*, 1976).

These reforms, which were intended to democratize the parties but in effect only succeeded in weakening them, are only the tip of the iceberg. Underlying them are changing political circumstances that have produced a more sophisticated electorate with less need for traditional political parties to clarify political issues and direct public debate. This more sophisticated electorate is the product of a new postindustrial, knowledge-centered economy in which, as David Apter, Daniel Bell, and others have maintained, the sale of services is replacing the sale of manufactured products. Noting these developments, Kevin Phillips—a onetime believer in the possibility of a Republican renaissance at the polls—now doubts whether any party is capable of capturing and organizing a voter realignment. In his book *Mediacracy* he contends that the growing knowledge elite has sought to modify and replace traditional political institutions, substituting its own modes of organization and methods of political communication in their place. Parties in a knowledge economy are, as Phillips argues, likely to become politically obsolete as the knowledge elite turns to the media to structure political information and clarify public issues. Already, he contends, in political campaigns "effective communications are replacing party organization as the key to political success."[27] Thus robbed of one of the main reasons for their existence—political education—traditional party organizations are likely to fade away.

Phillips' analysis is important because it appears to suggest that parties will not be easily revived even if immediate steps are taken to reverse prior reforms and to shore them up organizationally. Their accelerating decline implies that elections in the United States are likely to continue to be peripheral events instrumentally.

Public attitudes toward parties have in fact paralleled their objective decline as institutions of representation. As parties disintegrate, steep declines in public respect for parties have been recorded. These movements of opinion have been matched by dramatic increases in ticket switching and ticket splitting. In addition, there has been a progressive tendency for voters to disassociate themselves from identifying with either party, choosing instead to be "independents."

We may summarize the major findings of recent studies that document these changes. Data from the 1976 survey by the Michigan Center for Political Studies confirms the precipitous decline in public esteem for parties. In response to the question "Which part of the government on this list do you least often trust to do what's right?" 60 percent of respondents chose "political parties."[28] Conversely only 2 percent trust parties "to do what's right" (see Table 1). This trend is further documented by a group of colleagues led by Arthur Miller utilizing the same data. They reveal that the proportion of the electorate believing that "political parties help a good deal in making the government pay attention to what people think" dropped from 40 percent in 1964 to a new low of 17 percent in 1976 (see Table 2).[29]

Under the circumstances, it is only to be expected that voting according to professed party affiliation is breaking down. For many years, pioneers in the field of voting behavior, such as Angus Campbell, assumed that it was "normal" to vote according to one's party and that other factors such as candidate personality or the issues of the day caused only short-term deviations. In other words, it was assumed that the partisan vote was the normal vote.[30] These days it makes little sense for voters to assume that party voting will result in any predetermined set of policy consequences. Entrepreneurial candidates who have no long-term commitments to either party can adopt a party for the purposes of an election campaign, so citizens can no longer rely on the party label as a realistic guide to a candidate's future policy orientations. Voters can no longer indirectly endorse preferences or programs by choosing a Democrat rather than a Republican, since these labels cannot

Table 1

Responses to Question on Trust in Government, 1976[a]

Q: Which part of the government on this list do you most often trust to do what's right?

Congress	23%
Supreme Court	32%
President	24%
Parties	2%
All	2%
None	8%
Don't Know/ No answer	7%

Source: Data reprinted by permission from *American National Election Study, 1976* (machine-readable data file), conducted by the Center for Political Studies, the University of Michigan, under the direction of Warren E. Miller and Arthur H. Miller, ICPSR ed. (Ann Arbor, Mich.: Inter-university Consortium for Political and Social Research, 1977). Hereafter referred to in table source notes as *American National Election Study Series.*
[a] N = 2,403

guarantee a translation of campaign promises into policy outcomes. No wonder that partisan identification, once the main link in the chain connecting the citizen with the political process, has become a less important predictor of the vote. Increasingly citizens are tending to split their votes, that is, vote for one party at the presidential level and another at the congressional level. Outlining the massive proportions this phenomenon has reached, Lance Tarrance and Walter DeVries reveal that "until World War II more than 80% were ["straight ticket" voters]. Throughout the 1950s this statistic remained around 60–70%. . . . [But by 1968] more than half of those voting said they had split their ticket."[31] At last count, as reported in Arthur Miller's study of the 1976 presidential election, ticket splitting had reached new highs, particularly for the Republicans. Some 24 percent of Republicans had split their tickets in 1976, compared with only 10 percent in 1952. Even the Democrats, always more prone to split their tickets, did so 5 percent more than in 1952. And defections from party loyalty—ticket switching—are also on the increase. For example, in 1976, for the House of Representatives, the figures were as follows: 33 percent of Democrats and 43 percent of Republicans defected by voting for a party other than the one with which they had registered (see Table 3).[32]

Table 2

Responses to Question on Efficacy of Parties, 1964 and 1976

Q: How much do you feel that political parties help to make the government pay attention to what people think?

	1964[a]	1976[b]	Change
A good deal	40%	17%	−23%
Some	39%	52%	+13%
Not much	13%	25%	+12%
Don't know	7%	6%	−1%

Source: Date from *American National Study Series*, 1964; 1976.
[a] $N = 1,450$
[b] $N = 2,403$

Table 3

Responses to Question on Party-Line Voting, 1976[a]

Q: Have you always voted for the same party or have you voted for different parties for President?

Same party	37%
Different party	42%
Don't know/No answer	6%
Inappropriately coded	15%

Source: Data from *American National Election Study Series*, 1976.
[a] $N = 2,872$

Many voters are declining to identify with either party, choosing instead to become Independents. Gerald Pomper foresees "a non-partisan electoral future."

[The data] show that the proportion of independents has risen considerably and that the strength of partisanship has declined. They also reveal that this increase has occurred in all political generations and that it is greatest among the rising generations in the electorate. It is therefore quite likely that Independents will soon constitute a plurality of the nation.[33]

The latest figures indicate an increase in Independent voters to some 30 percent of the electorate, but the potential for an apartisan political future is reflected in Survey Research Center data, which indicate that in 1976 some 42 percent of the respondents interviewed saw no important differences between Republicans and Democrats (see Table 4). Comparing the 1972 and 1976 elections, Arthur Miller reluctantly confirms this trend:

> The reappearance of a strong direct effect of party identification on vote choice in 1976 does not necessarily imply that the trend toward weakening party loyalty evident in the U.S. since the mid-1960s has been arrested. On the contrary, evidence suggests that attitudes towards the parties have maintained their negative direction and that all attachments to the party system, when viewed more generally than vote choice alone, have continued to weaken.[34]

Under circumstances of party decline, some observers expect the rational voter to use issues as a voting cue rather than issues filtered through the prism of the now-tattered party label. Actually, however, voters are correct in behaving "irrationally" in also ignoring issues. There are two reasons for this. First, American political parties have never had a strong tradition of devising electoral agendas that had meaning beyond the campaign itself. In fact, the party platform is probably one of the least-read political docu-

Table 4

Responses to Question on Differences Between Parties, 1976[a]

Q: Do you think there are any important differences in what Democrats or Republicans stand for?

Yes	46%
No	42%
Don't Know	12%

Source: Data from *American National Election Study Series*, 1976.
[a] N = 2,871

ments—by voters or by candidates! Even Gerald Pomper, long a defender of party platforms and their significance for policy, was forced to acknowledge that only 27 percent of platform statements are specific enough to be considered "pledges." Moreover, he admits that only "about a tenth of all pledges involve party conflict."[35] If this is so, meaningful programmatic choices are not possible.

To the extent that there are platform differences, we should keep in mind the nature of the differences and where they emanate from. Above all, they do not represent a coherent approach to political-economic issues by party regulars. Instead, they represent the efforts of zealous interest groups who have become important constituencies of their respective parties and who have been able to dominate platform writing on their specific issue. Thus this trend exemplifies the disarray of parties, since the issues do not necessarily represent the broad thinking of party members and their constituencies at large.[36]

Party platforms are either too broad to be meaningfully programmatic or too narrow for mass appeal. Under such circumstances, presidential (as well as other) candidates for the most part have chosen to ignore party platforms and to mount personal campaigns with the help of professional campaign managers whose only concern is winning. Hence there is a tendency to avoid specific issues and to emphasize instead vague slogans that serve to create name recognition and a favorable overall image.

Indeed, as far as congressional campaigns are concerned, David Mayhew emphasized that "advertising one's name so as to create name recognition and a brand image, as it were, has become a mandatory exercise."[37] The focus of such advertising must draw attention to personal qualities such as "experience" or "sincerity," avoiding specific issues. In principle, offering voters a choice between candidates which focuses on their personal competence rather than on issues could be viewed as a rational one—but for the fact that a candidate's competence is a chimera, a creation of his or her professional campaign managers. All too often, campaign managers are media or public relations experts, such as David Garth and Joe Napolitan. Occasionally issues do creep into election campaigns, but as Mayhew cynically observes, this is only an exercise in position-taking for effect. No one, least of all the candidate, expects those positions to be translated into public policy. Hence current electoral contests have been characterized as games of political skill and technique between teams of nonideological professionals whose task is complete once the election tallies are counted.

Despite this, some observers (e.g., Sidney Verba, Norman Nie, and John

Petrocik) have claimed to see the beginnings of issue-oriented presidential elections, naming 1964 as a crucial transition year: "That is the year when the public becomes more issue-oriented and its issue-positions develop a coherence they did not previously have. At the same time citizens begin voting consistently with their issue positions."[38] The conclusions of such astute political observers demand to be placed in context, however. To be sure, presidential candidates are more hard-pressed than others seeking public office to articulate issues of national concern and to provide a persuasive raison d'être for entering the presidential race.

Nevertheless, presidential candidates, frequently cast adrift from ties to their party's platform and in the course of an entrepreneurial campaign, increasingly using television as the communication medium of choice, have found it difficult to infuse their campaigns with a clear thematic focus. Frequently that focus comes to rest on subliminal character issues. In 1960, John Kennedy's "youth" (what Richard Nixon called his "immaturity and impulsiveness") and his "religion" became important issues. Twenty years later the focus was on his brother Edward Kennedy's "moral fitness for office" as well as on Jimmy Carter's "competence" and Ronald Reagan's "age."

At other times an apparent focus on substantive issues has become deflected into peripheral concerns that drift in and out of campaigns. For instance, the status of Quemoy and Matsu surfaced surprisingly in the 1960 televised debates between Nixon and Kennedy, while in 1976 Reagan brought up the Panama Canal issue, thereby attracting much media and public attention.

Alternatively, broad thematic generalizations may come to dominate presidential campaigns, substituting for more clearly focused substantive concerns. John Kennedy's pledge to "get the country moving again," Richard Nixon's focus on "law and order" in 1968, or Jimmy Carter's post-Watergate "politics of love" motif in 1976 (and his subsequent pledge in his acceptance speech to "make the government as decent and competent as its people") all serve to exemplify this trend. When substantive issues of national concern do emerge, they are not part of an organizationally coherent network but are frequently raised in an eclectic fashion, even to the point where they may mislead the public. For instance, Lyndon Johnson's identification with peace (as opposed to his opponent, Barry Goldwater, who was characterized as "trigger happy") was followed by a massive buildup of the Vietnam War. In 1980 Jimmy Carter's attempt to inject the important issue of nuclear proliferation into his campaign followed his prior authorization of a uranium sale to India, a country that had just exploded a nuclear device. And despite Carter's defense of the SALT II treaty in his televised debates with Ronald Reagan in 1980, the President had earlier backed off on the issue, concluding that it lacked the necessary two-thirds majority in the Senate. After the Iran crisis exploded, Carter found it more expedient to push for an increase in defense spending and to postpone his drive for Senate ratification of the treaty, picking it up later when it seemed expedient to do so.[39]

All in all, in political campaigns there is no consistently expressed programmatic issue-content equivalent to the platforms presented, for instance, to French or British voters by candidates seeking public office under the banner of organizational strong parties. All too frequently political information is presented to voters in the form of brief but expensive campaign commercials that are about as informative as commercials for soap that use the advertising strategy of comparing one product with another. One commercial, aired during Gerald Ford's abortive bid for reelection in 1976, showed two women outside a supermarket discussing Ford's attributes in precisely those terms. Television trivializes what little potential exists for serious political discussion of the "issues." Moreover, televised debates, potentially a more suitable forum for a serious discussion of the issues than commercials, are limited both in number and in time, due in part to the Federal Communications Commission's "equal time" rule. The equal-time rule requires television stations to give equivalent air time to all political candidates seeking a particular office—something the networks are reluctant to do since it would disrupt regular programming schedules and lead to a possible loss of commercial revenues.

In any case, given the disorganization of parties, the dearth of serious issues goes beyond the format of campaign debate, as we have already indicated. Despite this, journalists have a tendency to label certain politicians as "issue" candidates. In recent decades, for instance, Barry Goldwater, George McGovern, Eugene McCarthy, and John Anderson have been tagged with this label. On closer examination of the context of their campaigns, it becomes apparent that this designation is immensely misleading. All these so-called issue candidates have had to devise ad hoc election campaigns, and the issues on which they chose to focus reflect this.

In Goldwater's case, issue content was difficult to find at all. For example, Theodore White, a highly respected chronicler of presidential election campaigns emphasized the emotional rather than the rational, policy-oriented aspects of Goldwater's campaign. In *The Making of the President*

1964 White observed: "Goldwater could offer—and this was his greatest contribution to American politics—only a contagious concern. . . . He caused nerve ends to twinge with his passion and indignation. Yet he had no *handle to the problems, no program and no solution.*"[40]

George McGovern, perceived as one of the most issue-oriented candidates ever to seek the presidency, initially appeared to have taken specific positions in three substantive areas: defense, the economy, and welfare. During the course of the campaign, however, McGovern was forced to back away from his initial specificity. It had become clear that his proposals not only were alienating many voters but also, more important, were not as carefully articulated as had they been portrayed by a press anxious to explain McGovern's meteoric rise. Theodore White again provides revealing insight into the haphazard manner in which McGovern's platform was pasted together. One of the three major planks, the lowering of the defense budget, was authored by a young lawyer, John Holum, and White commented, "As the thesis of a young Ph.D. student it would have been outstanding. But Holum was tackling the most complicated problem of American survival and his action recommendation as a package did not make sense."[41] White was even more disparaging about the controversial "economics program" featuring "Great Issue No. 3—the $1,000 giveaway":

If the defense program of George McGovern had John Holum as its identifiable father, if it had the rational control of one mind exerting itself to bring order out of a stack of handouts and newspaper clippings, the same could not be said of the McGovern Economics Program. . . . No one ever throughout the campaign wanted to acknowledge fatherhood [of that].[42]

In the 1980 presidential campaign, John Anderson was touted as the "idea" candidate, the thinking person's alternative to the lackluster choices provided by the two major parties. His campaign manager, David Garth, promised a campaign of issues: "The focus will be on issues. There won't be any music or bands playing behind him and a lot of hoopla. They don't have any place in an issue-oriented campaign."[43] As a practical matter, however, Anderson's campaign soon became bogged down in the technicalities of getting on the ballot, and the ad hoc nature of his campaign was reflected in a later comment by Garth: "There is no blueprint on this one. Our approach will be to take it step by step."[44] As "the candidate with a difference," Anderson ultimately was able to raise only three disconnected issues for public debate: federally financed abortions, registration of handguns, and a

50-cent-per-gallon gasoline tax, hardly sufficient to present voters with a clear alternative, despite Anderson's shrill insistence to the contrary. One observer noted that the emperor had no clothes: "It's one thing to stand up for the grain embargo, push for a gas tax and abortion, but there's not a whole lot there."[45] Moreover, even Anderson's image as a liberal on the social issues appeared to be contradicted by his eclectic voting record in Congress, where he had voted over the years against foreign aid, Medicare, food stamps, federal aid to education, and federal aid to the arts and humanities.[46]

Since elections, even at the highest levels, do not offer citizens meaningful choices among coherent programs, it is appropriate and only fitting that the people have chosen to make their electoral choices on some other basis. We know that voters are capable of behaving rationally and instrumentally, since they do so when engaging in other participatory activities as well as in the course of their lives. During elections, however, given a context of party decline and issue avoidance by candidates, the only available differences are those of personality, and even those are contrived. The alternatives offered to voters thus leave them little choice but to vote "irrationally."

Do Voters Make Retrospective Judgments?

We noted earlier a second tendency misperceived as being "irrational," namely, that voters increasingly refuse to exercise their rights to "vote the rascals out," to punish politicians, and thereby to enforce political control. Much of the journal literature confirms that voters ignore results. The growing tendency to reelect incumbents instead is demonstrated, for instance, by the findings of Albert Cover. Between 1956 and 1976, an astonishing 90 percent of incumbents were reelected, on average, to the House of Representatives.[47] Senate races have shown a similar increase in the advantages of incumbency. In a study entitled "Party and Incumbency in the Post-War Senate Elections," Warren Kostroski states as his major finding: "The relative importance of parties and incumbency in Senate elections has changed drastically over the last quarter century. Party has undergone an overall decline in influence while incumbency has experienced a roughly proportionate increase."[48] This trend appears to have accelerated, with 96 percent of incumbents being returned to Congress in 1978. Of even greater significance is that voters are prepared to switch party loyalties in order to support an incumbent of the rival party.[49] Even in the 1980 elections, widely regarded as punishing to incumbents, especially Democrats, and despite the losses of several name Democrats, such as George McGovern, Frank Church, and Birch Bayh, two-thirds of senators seeking reelection won, while in the House less than 10 percent of representatives lost (38 out of 435).[50]

Even when the White House changes hands, the electoral chances of incumbent senators and congresspersons appear to be unaffected. As Lloyd Cutler and Douglas Dillon indicate, when President Carter lost in 1980, some 231 out of 268 Democrats in the House and Senate were reelected, even from districts that Carter himself did not carry. That this is not an exception to the rule can be seen clearly in the four preceding presidential elections, in which party control of the White House changed hands but incumbent senators and congresspersons were reelected.[51]

Year	Senators and Congresspersons Reelected in Years When President of Same Party Lost
1952 (D)	187/208
1960 (R)	142/145
1968 (D)	246/257
1976 (R)	125/134

Incumbents have been receiving ever larger shares of special-interest monies donated through political action committees. In 1982, for example, 66.7 percent of political action committee donations went to incumbents, as opposed to 61.2 percent in 1980, thus magnifying the advantages of incumbency.[52] Why are voters choosing not to "vote the rascals out" as much of the time as democratic theory suggests they should? One reason is that retrospective voting can be meaningfully practiced only when results can be attributed to one candidate or party. When political accountability is difficult to assign, it is appropriate that voters avoid doing so.

As a result of the organizational weakness of parties in the legislature and the realities of institutional fragmentation which divide a president from his own party, policy (when it gets made) tends to be the outcome of shifting coalitions and endless compromises which blur lines of political responsibility. An early study by Randall Ripley and Lewis Froman of House Democrats in 1963 (important because the Democrats at the time had not only a majority but also a President of the same party, and because party unity voting was unusually high) found that, despite the authors' initial presumption that "the single most important variable explaining legislature outcomes is party organization," party unity voting was in fact most likely to occur on procedural issues of low visibility where there were few counterpressures from the constituency or from state delegations.[53] Under pressure and on substantive issues, House Democrats had little incentive to toe the party line and on many occasions did not do so, Southern Democrats being the most likely to defect.

Over the past decade, regional defections resulting in coalition voting have tended to increase in frequency, resulting in even lower rates of party unity. Barbara Sinclair's contributions on this point are especially noteworthy, since she has written extensively about the consequences of critical elections when party unity was high and policy outcomes apparently nonincremental. In a recent article entitled "Who Wins in the House of Representatives: The Effects of Declining Party Cohesion on Policy Outputs: 1959–1970," she identifies four regional segments: Northern Democrats, Southern Democrats, Eastern Republicans, and non-Eastern Republicans. Increasingly during this period she finds that Southern Democrats have defected from the Democratic fold to vote alongside non-Eastern Republicans. On the other hand, the majority segment of the Democratic party has become increasingly dependent on the support of Eastern Republicans to achieve victory. Sinclair herself concludes that these developments mean that "since the majority segment of the majority party is not large enough to win without allies, the two minority segments to a large extent determine outcomes."[54]

Blurring the lines of political responsibility still further is the incidence of bipartisan voting in which a majority of voting Republicans and Democrats vote in agreement. It happens twice as often as party unity voting, occurring 61 percent of the time in the Senate and 64 percent of the time in the House between 1967 and 1977.[55]

Hence there is no easy way for voters to distinguish the records of either party and to punish or reward candidates bearing their respective party labels. These developments, however, do not in and of themselves explain why voters consistently are choosing to reelect incumbents over challengers. An explanation for the underlying rationality of their decisions must be sought in the changing political roles that congresspeople have come to play and in the adaptation of public expectations of what it is that congresspeople are supposed to do.

They are not expected to be decision-makers first and foremost. Given the growth of the regulatory/administrative arm of government and the changing locus of decision-making power, Morris Fiorina creatively argues that congresspeople are now expected to assume the role of ombudsmen whose primary duty is to serve constituency needs.⁵⁶ As intermediaries, they provide citizens with contacts in agencies and bureaus. Indeed, Theodore Lowi maintains, "Congressional parties are built manifestly to perform constituent functions and not to perform—indeed to avoid performing—policy functions."⁵⁷ That being the case, the emphasis in Congress has shifted from the controversial (taking positions on national issues) to the noncontroversial (providing individual favors for constituents).

Under these circumstances, what counts most with constituents is a congressperson's experience in office. Hence it makes little sense for voters to turn out a politician with connections and seniority and replace him or her with a neophyte. Consequently incumbents continue to gain reelection at an increasing rate. In fact, voters frequently spurn the opportunity to eject even corrupt (but experienced) politicians (the reelection of Daniel Flood being a good example) and will discount even credible information of a candidate's misdeeds. In one case, that of black representative Charles Diggs, recently censured by the House and stripped of his committee chairmanships for taking part in a payroll kickback scheme, loyal constituents remain staunchly convinced that congressional action was motivated solely by racism. Shedding additional light on this, a study by Barry Rundquist and his colleagues implies that the corrupt politician may be immune from voter reprisal because voters tend to trade off that information for other things they value in candidates,⁵⁸ and they may well value his corruptibility.

In fact, doing favors for constituents (even for money) is probably perceived by many people as part of a public official's job, the post-Watergate moral climate notwithstanding. And the recent evidence of "Operation Abscam" in 1980 (in which FBI agents posed as wealthy Arabs willing to pay large sums for special favors) indicates that many public officials, when contacted through such direct channels, may be only too eager to perform that aspect of their jobs. In any case, to say that the "errand boy" function of representatives is now the most important one is to admit that their political role has radically changed from the one contemplated for them by democratic theory—to be the nation's primary decision-makers.

In conclusion, it is not necessary to prove that citizens vote rationally to prove that they are rational. Given an electoral system that provides few opportunities for instrumental behavior, it makes more sense for voters to make uninformed choices and to reserve their instrumental orientations for other types of participatory acts in the political arena which are more likely than voting to yield them tangible benefits. The next chapter will consider in more detail the extraelectoral channels that have come to play a major role in contemporary American politics and to examine nonelectoral modes of participatory behavior.

Notes

1. Gerald Pomper, *Elections in America: Control and Influence in Democratic Politics* (New York: Dodd, Mead & Co., 1968), p. 67 (emphasis added). See also Benjamin Ginsberg, *The Consequences of Consent* (Addison-Wesley, 1981).
2. Morris Fiorina, *Retrospective Voting in American Elections* (New Haven: Yale University Press, 1981), p. 6.
3. Pomper, *Elections in America*, p. 254.
4. See Anthony Downs, *An Economic Theory of Democracy* (New York: Harper & Row, 1957), chap. 12.
5. See Bernard Berelson, Paul Lazarfeld, and William McPhee, *Voting* (Chicago: University of Chicago Press, 1954).
6. Michael Shapiro, "Rational Political Man: A Synthesis of Economic and Social Psychological Perspectives," *American Political Science Review* 63 (December 1969): 1106.
7. Michael Margolis, "From Confusion to Confusion: Issues and the American Voter, 1955–1972," *American Political Science Review* 71 (1977): 32.
8. Gerald Pomper and Mark Schulman, "Variability in American Electoral Behavior: Longitudinal Perspectives from Causal Modeling," *American Journal of Political Science* 19 (February 1975): 1–18. See also Pomper et al., "From Confusion to Clarity: Issues and the American Voter," *American Political Science Review* 66 (June 1972): 415–28.
9. David E. RePass, "Issue Salience and Party Choice," *American Political Science Review* 45 (June 1971): 389–400.
10. Arthur Miller et al., "Partisanship Reinstated? A Comparison of the 1972 and 1976 Presidential Elections," *British Journal of Political Science* 58 (April 1978): 144.
11. Ibid., p. 136.
12. V. O. Key, *The Responsible Electorate* (Cambridge: Belknap Press of Harvard University, 1966).
13. Pomper and Schulman, "Variability in American Electoral Behavior," pp. 1–18.
14. Norman Nie, Sidney Verba, and John Petrocik, *The Changing American Voter* (Cambridge: Harvard University Press, 1976), p. 145. Emphasis added.
15. Margolis, "From Confusion to Confusion," p. 32.

16. Ibid., p. 34.
17. George Bishop et al., "Changing Structure of Mass Belief Systems: Fact or Artifact," *Journal of Politics* 40 (August 1978): 782–87. See also George Bishop, Alfred Tuchfarber, and Robert Oldendick, "Change in the Structure of American Political Attitudes: The Nagging Question of Question Wording," *American Journal of Political Science* 22 (May 1978): 250–69.
18. John L. Sullivan, James E. Piereson, and George E. Marcus, "Ideological Constraint in the Mass Public: A Methodological Critique and Some New Findings," *American Journal of Political Science* 22 (May 1978): 247.
19. See Edward Carmines and James A. Stimson, "The Two Faces of Issue Voting," *American Political Science Review* 74 (March 1980): 78–91.
20. Dennis M. Anderson, "Voting and Misvoting on the Ohio Election Day Registration Referendum," Paper presented at the Ohio Association of Economists and Political Scientists, Worthington, Ohio, March 1979. We must emphasize that Anderson himself chose to stress the extent of misvoting. See also Raymond E. Wolfinger and Fred I. Greenstein, "The Repeal of Fair Housing in California: An Analysis of Referendum Voting," *American Political Science Review* 62 (September 1968): 753–69.
21. Walter Dean Burnham, *Critical Elections* (New York: W. W. Norton & Co., 1970), p. 9.
22. Barbara Sinclair, "Policy Consequences of Party Realignment: Social Welfare Legislation in the House of Representatives," *American Journal of Political Science* 22 (February 1978): 102. See also Barbara Sinclair, "Party Realignment and the Transformation of the Political Agenda: The House of Representatives, 1925–1938," *American Political Science Review* 71 (September 1977): 940–53.
23. Walter Dean Burnham, "Revitalization and Decay: Looking Towards the Third Century of American Electoral Politics," *Journal of Politics* 38 (August 1976): 149. See also "American Politics in the 1980s—Beyond Party?" in *The American Party System,* ed. William N. Chambers and Walter Dean Burnham, 2d ed. (New York: Oxford University Press, 1975), pp. 308–57. See also V. O. Key, Jr., "A Theory of Critical Elections," *Journal of Politics* 17 (February 1955): 3–18.
24. E. E. Schattschneider, *Party Government* (New York: Farrah & Rinehart, 1942), p. 32.
25. Austin Ranney, *Curing the Mischiefs of Faction: Party Reform in America* (Berkeley: University of California Press, 1975), p. 3.
26. Gerald Pomper, "The Decline of the Party in American Elections," *Political Science Quarterly* 92 (Spring 1977): 21–42. See also "Impacts on the Political System," *American Politics Quarterly* 3 (July 1975): 348. Pomper's earlier confidence in political parties was expressed in his *Elections in America*.

Many states (27 by 1984) have chosen the caucus method of selecting delegates. Others have selected the primary (25 in 1984). Since the 1972 rules changes (and despite changes in 1982), activists rather than party regulars dominate.

27. Kevin Phillips, *Mediacracy* (Garden City, N.Y.: Doubleday & Co., 1975), p. v.
28. See *American National Election Study Series 1976* (Machine-readable data file), conducted by the Center for Political Studies, the University of Michigan, under the direction of Warren E. Miller and Arthur H. Miller. ICPSR ed. Ann Arbor, Mich.: Inter-university Consortium for Political and Social Research, 1977.
29. Miller et al., "Partisanship Reinstated?" p. 129.
30. See Angus Campbell et al., *Voting* (New York: John Wiley & Sons, 1960).
31. Lance Tarrance and Walter DeVries, *The Ticket Splitters* (Grand Rapids: Wm. B. Eerdmans Publishing Co., 1972), p. 22.
32. Miller, "Partisanship Reinstated?" p. 132.
33. Pomper, "Decline of the Party," p. 36.
34. Miller et al., "Partisanship Reinstated?" p. 131.
35. Pomper, *Elections in America*, pp. 182, 193.
36. The 1980 election also demonstrated the irresponsible nature of platform writing since the Democrats (doubtless to appease Ted Kennedy) passed an economic platform that implicitly repudiated the record of their own incumbent President, whom they had just renominated.
37. David Mayhew, *Congress: The Electoral Connection* (New Haven: Yale University Press, 1974), p. 62.
38. Nie, Verba, and Petrocik, *The Changing American Voter*, p. 307.
39. *National Journal*, November 1, 1980, p. 1852.
40. Theodore White, *The Making of the President 1964* (New York: New American Library, 1966), p. 314. Emphasis added.
41. Theodore White, *The Making of the President 1972* (New York: Atheneum Books, 1973), p. 117.
42. Ibid.
43. David Garth, quoted in the *National Journal*, May 17, 1980, p. 806.
44. Ibid.
45. Aide to President Jimmy Carter, quoted in ibid., p. 810.
46. *Congressional Quarterly Almanac 1968*, p. 943.
47. Albert D. Cover, "One Good Term Deserves Another: The Advantage of Incumbency in Congressional Elections," *American Journal of Political Science* 21 (August 1977): 523–41. For a historical comparison, see H. Douglas Price, "The Congressional Career: Then and Now," *Congressional Behavior*, ed. Nelson W. Polsby (New York: Random House, 1971), pp. 14–27.
48. See Warren Lee Kostroski, "Party and Incumbency in Post-War Senate Elec-

tions," *American Political Science Review* 67 (December 1973): 1213–34. Kostroski calculates that at other levels incumbency rates are similarly high—e.g., city councilpersons succeed at the rate of 80 percent and state legislators between 70 and 90 percent. For the presidency, no incumbent President who has chosen to run (with the exception of Herbert Hoover and Gerald Ford) has ever lost. Only gubernatorial elections appear to be relatively competitive; 64.7 percent of incumbents are reelected.
49. See Cover, "One Good Term," p. 525.
50. The extent to which voters even consider highly salient economic issues in casting a retrospective vote is not clear. Gerald Kramer (1971) concluded that economic fluctuations have an important influence, whereas Stigler (1973) concluded that they do not. The debate continues with James Kuklinski and Darrell M. West (1981) arguing that it occurs in Senate but not in House elections, Ray Fair arguing that it occurs in presidential elections (1978), and D. Roderick Kiewiet (1981) arguing broadly that voters concerned with unemployment lean toward Democratic candidates, while those concerned with inflation vote Republican. Kuklinski and West warn, however, that "there is no guarantee that the public will influence the direction of macro-economic policy."
51. Lloyd N. Cutler and C. Douglas Dillon, "Can We Improve Our Constitutional System?" *Wall Street Journal*, February 15, 1983, p. 32.
52. *Wall Street Journal*, April 29, 1983, p. 20. By 1983, Congress Watch, an organization sponsored by Ralph Nader, calculated that 92% of P.A.C. contributions went to incumbent House and Senate members.
53. Lewis Froman and Randall Ripley, "Conditions for Party Leadership: The Case of the House Democrats," *American Political Science Review* 59 (March 1965): 52–63. This was not always the case. High levels of party voting were recorded for the early part of this century by E. W. Brady and P. Althoff in "Party Voting and the House of Representatives 1890–1910: Elements of a Responsible Two-party System," *Journal of Politics* 36 (August 1974): 771.
54. Barbara Sinclair, "Who Wins in the House of Representatives: The Effects of Declining Party Cohesion on Policy Outputs, 1959–1970," *Social Science Quarterly* 58 (June 1977): 128.
55. See *Congressional Quarterly Almanac*, 1967–77.
56. Morris Fiorina, "The Case of the Vanishing Marginals: The Bureaucracy Did It," *American Political Science Review* 71 (March 1977): 177–81. Earlier arguments had suggested that politicians go unpunished simply because citizens are unaware and ignorant of their records. Warren E. Miller and Donald E. Stokes, "Constituency Influence in Congress," *American Political Science Review* 57 (March 1963): 55–65, had indicated that the "constituency's awareness of

the policy stands of the representative is ordinarily slight." See also Charles F. Cnudde and Donald McCrone, "The Linkage Between Constituency Attitudes and Congressional Voting Behavior," *American Political Science Review* 72 (March 1966): 66–72.

57. See Theodore Lowi, *The End of Liberalism*, 2d ed. (New York: W. W. Norton & Co., 1979), p. 55. A similar argument is made by Barbara Deckard and John Stanley, "Party Decomposition and Reform in the House of Representatives," *Western Political Quarterly* 27 (January 1974): 249–64.

58. See Barry S. Rundquist, Gerald Strom, and John Peters, "Corrupt Politicians and Their Electoral Support: Some Experimental Observations," *American Political Science Review* 71 (September 1977): 954–63.

THREE

Extra-Electoral Participatory Activity

This chapter will describe the developments external to the electoral process which have tended to shift the center of decision-making gravity toward outcomes determined by judicial and bureaucratic politics rather than by electoral politics. The shift has occurred even though the U.S. Constitution seemed to mandate a representative model of democracy by naming Congress as the legislative branch, admitting the President into the lawmaking process only through a complex system of overlapping authorities. We will argue that, despite the major role of the President in initiating policy, Congress has neither the political inclination nor the legislative capability to respond adequately to public demands on it, preferring instead to delegate many important issues to judicial and bureaucratic disposition. This trend will not be easily reversed.

This chapter will also describe the extent to which citizen influence and control increasingly occur through participatory activities directed at extra-electoral channels whose availability serves to compensate for the vitiation of electoral linkages. Indeed, this "participation explosion" that some observers have alluded to (which includes citizen-initiated contacts and public interest group activity) seems to indicate that citizens have chosen to ignore Joseph Schumpeter's dictum that in a representative democracy "the voters

... must respect the division of labor between themselves and the politicians they elect. ... They must understand that once they have elected an individual, political action is his business, not theirs."[1] We will show that such extra-electoral participatory activity is undertaken instrumentally, in marked contrast with the way citizens vote.

Much of this direct participatory activity has been government-initiated through legislative mandating of citizen participation in administrative decisions and encouraged by the judiciary, which has overturned prior impediments to public participation by expansion of basic constitutional concepts such as legal standing and due process. Taken together, these precedents that have enabled continuous citizen involvement will be difficult to abandon, even if the responsibility for governance could be returned exclusively to the elected branches.

The Makers of Public Policy

Electoral myth, based on the precepts of democratic theory, identified the elected branches as the principal policymakers, and public policy as largely campaign-defined. At the present time, considerable soul-searching attends this point of view, but in the recent past this myth has dominated the consensus perspective. By way of illustration, note the conclusions of a now-classic exposition of this perspective: "In our studies of presidential and gubernatorial elections we found that the initiatives and commitments of parties and candidates *are vital in the determination of public policy*. . . . These initiatives as expressed in national party platforms have been relatively specific and related to the apparent interests of the citizenry."[2] To buttress claims of a linkage between elections and public policy, Gerald Pomper undertook an extensive content analysis of party platforms from 1944 to 1964 and traced their metamorphosis into law. His finding that half of all platform pledges were converted into policy was apparently encouraging enough for him to conclude that "elections do make a difference . . . by installing a coalition with specific commitments . . . [which are] likely of fulfillment."[3] Despite Pomper's sanguinity, it would be difficult to call any other contract significantly fulfilled if only half done—for example, a contract to buy a car, build a house, or write a book. Even so, subsequent efforts to establish links between elections and public policy also claimed success. For instance, Benjamin Ginsberg examined the party platforms of both the

Democrats and the Republicans from 1844 to 1968, as well as all laws passed by Congress between 1789 and 1968. He discovered significant differences between the platforms of the two parties during certain periods (1856, 1880, 1896, and 1932) and, concurrently, many new laws were passed.[4] These studies may be encouraging for some, but only as far as they go. To determine accurately the influence elections have on public policy, we must not merely determine the proportion of the party platform converted into public policy but also assess the extent to which public policy *in toto* is derived from party platforms.

The Diminishing Roles of Congress and the President

We shall consider separately the three phases involved in the policy-making process: initiation, enactment, and implementation. Since the Truman era, the President has emerged as the major initiator of legislative proposals, and it is he who, on assuming office, oversees the creation of the nation's publicized agenda. But it is the exception rather than the rule that campaign promises (or, given the entrepreneurial nature of the presidential quest, the party platform) constitute a major source on which the President draws for his proposals. Much of the President's campaign rhetoric was comprised of the recommendations of hastily convened advisory task forces or based on quick consultations with experts. So the legislative agenda is likely to be defined only after the campaign is over, victory at the polls seldom being based on any coherent program.

For policy guidance once in office, presidents have tended to rely either on task forces made up of outside experts, as Kennedy and Johnson did initially,[5] or on cabinet secretaries and bureau chiefs from within the executive branch. Richard Nixon and, later, Gerald Ford attempted to centralize and direct this process through the Executive Office with the creation of the Domestic Council and the reorganization of the Bureau of the Budget into the Office of Management and Budget, while Jimmy Carter deemphasized the White House role further with the creation of his own Domestic Policy Staff.[6]

Nevertheless, in devising a legislative agenda the President remains enmeshed within a bureaucratic spider's web, on which he must rely for the policy ideas he presents to Congress. As a result, electoral agendas are frequently ignored, if not bypassed. The process by which legislative agendas are developed helps to explain why a president may bring up important items for congressional consideration which actually run contrary to specific policy statements on his own party's platform. Carter's about-face on oil price decontrol—of immense importance in its effects—is an example. The issue of controls on oil had initially and unexpectedly been placed on the legislative agenda of the Democratic Congress by a Republican president, Richard Nixon.

In 1971, Nixon confounded conventional wisdom and his own party's 1968 platform, which had promised that "a Republican Administration will ... avoid such distortions as wage and price controls"[7] and unilaterally imposed wage and price controls in order to fight inflation. Oil price controls had been included as part of this package. In 1973, however, Congress approved continuing such controls as part of the Emergency Petroleum Allocation Act and later as part of the 1975 Energy Policy and Conservation Act.

The maintenance of oil price controls subsequently became an important plank on the Democratic party platform of 1976. That platform had referred to the 1975 act as a "direct result of the Democratic Congress's commitment to the principle that beyond certain levels, increasing energy prices simply produces high-cost energy—without producing any additional energy supplies."[8] The Democrats in effect endorsed a policy of continuing oil price controls. However, since the act had provided for controls to end in 1979, the issue was again placed on the legislative agenda, this time by President Carter. It was by no means in the form prescribed by his own party platform. On the contrary, Carter proposed to Congress that it end oil price controls, and despite the vigorous protests of Representative Toby Moffett in the House and Senator Henry Jackson in the Senate, Carter's plan for decontrol of oil prices went into effect.

Frequently, then, the electoral process is short-circuited, so that items are brought up for consideration without ever having gone through the electoral process. A recent study by John Bacheller confirms this. He found that by "far the greatest number" of items brought to the legislature were raised and defined by organized segments of the public operating through the executive branch. On the other hand, he found that relatively few of the issues he studied (35 percent) were "campaign defined," even though the public salience of such issues, since they involved controversial areas such as civil rights, health, and welfare, was much higher.[9] Thus while there is a perception that the electoral agenda is crucial, reality suggests otherwise.

A secondary source of legislative initiatives can be traced to a handful of activist senators, representatives being generally too preoccupied with seeking reelection to contribute much. Jack Walker has identified such senatorial activists as political entrepreneurs whose agendas are personal and whose alliances are temporary rather than institutionalized (i.e., organized around parties).[10] Their legislative initiatives may be frustrated for years or, infrequently, may become law. An example of the former is Senator Birch Bayh's decade-long bid for a constitutional amendment to abolish the electoral college and award the presidency to the candidate with the largest popular vote. On the other hand, successful legislative initiatives pushed through by other senators include the Taft-Hartley Act of 1947, the Smith Act of 1940, and the Humphrey-Hawkins Full Employment Act of 1978.

There are a few instances where the legislative initiatives of activist senators and congresspeople may ex post facto become a source of campaign dialogue. Senator Edward Kennedy sponsored his own national health insurance plan while in the Senate and later took it with him on the campaign trail when he sought the presidency in 1980. On the Republican side, the Kemp-Roth proposal to slash federal taxes was a strong plank on Ronald Reagan's personal presidential platform, and one generally endorsed by his party.

That a variant of the Kemp-Roth proposal appeared on the legislative agenda of Congress within a few weeks of Reagan's electoral victory in 1980 is generally conceded to be the exception rather than the rule. In general, congresspeople who devise policy initiatives for campaign consumption do so individually, to ensure their personal electoral survival. Ordinarily such initiatives are not expected to pass. As David Mayhew indicated, "The Congressman as a position-taker is a speaker rather than a doer. The electoral requirement is not that he make pleasing things happen but that he make pleasing judgmental statements."[11] In any event, the weight of the evidence seems to suggest that since electoral agendas are only tenuously and occasionally related to legislative agendas, party platforms cannot be considered a major source of public policy, nor can the often uninformed and vague campaign promises of presidential candidates.

Turning now to the question of policy enactment, one can readily see that the process is painstakingly slow and extremely arduous. Each session, Congress is able to enact only a small proportion of its legislative agenda. How small a proportion is indicated by the following figures compiled by the *Congressional Quarterly Almanac*. In 1977, some 15,386 bills and resolutions were introduced, of which only 233 were cleared and signed by the President. Of these, only 11 could be considered of major significance. Even so, several important and controversial issues such as national health insurance and energy policy were left unresolved.[12]

Several factors impede legislative progress. Given the weakness of party control, legislative discipline is impossible to enforce. Indeed, as Mayhew suggests, party leaders recognize that congresspeople should be left free to take positions that serve their own, not their party's, electoral advantage. Given the needs of its members in this respect, "The best service a party can supply to its congressmen is a negative one; it can leave them alone. . . . The fact is that enactment of party programs is electorally not very important to members (although some may find it important to take positions on programs)."[13]

Moreover, the very structure of Congress, marked as it is by an extensive committee system that multiplies the possibilities for delay and interbranch conflict, is designed to throw roadblocks in the way of rapid policy enactment. Add to this lack of legislative will and the structurally imposed conflict a paucity of expertise in certain areas of legislation, and Congress, despite fervent efforts to fulfill its constitutional responsibilities, emerges as an undependable policymaker.

As a result, we are witnessing a relative decline in the policy-making responsibilities of Congress and a shift to other equally important but nonpolicy roles. Congress still does retain an important symbolic role in setting forth broad guidelines and parameters for the future direction of policy, but George Shipman urges us to be cautious in assessing Congress's policy role:

Legislative enactments seem to be largely ceremonial in many instances. . . . What the legislature does do is authorize and legitimize a search . . . for a set of impacts agreeable to interested groups in the society. In other words, *legislation is more a charter for undertaking policy formation than it is for policy making in any conclusive sense.*[14]

Shipman's cautionary note in interpreting the significance of what Congress does pass is highlighted by what the *Congressional Quarterly* colorfully calls "the legislative grand slam" enacted by the 89th Congress under the tutelage of President Lyndon Johnson. Despite the unusually broad (if eclectic) sweep of legislation, much of it was hastily considered, Congress having been instructed to approve the bills presented to it and worry about perfecting details later. Senate Majority Leader Mike Mansfield, making a statement at a Democratic conference meeting soon afterward, was so concerned about this that he urged that Congress's second session in 1966 be devoted to "the perfection, the elaboration and the refinement of the basic legislation which underpins major federal programs and particularly the legislation which has been put into the statute books during the past three or four years."[15] Mansfield's admonition to the Congress to further spell out its legislative enactments was ignored as legislators' time became occupied with other more pressing tasks such as the Vietnam War and the deteriorating economy. Fifteen years later, Barber Conable, U.S. Representative from New York, recalled this tendency in an interview: "Every day we were identifying a new national problem and solving it by ordering the President to solve it and then giving him 35 cents to do it."[16] David Mayhew explains why: Since electoral payment is for positions taken rather than for effects, the tendency is for Congress to produce "statutes that are long on goals but short on means to achieve them."[17]

Other additional responsibilities now serve to divert congressional attention. For instance, Congress's investigatory function has been enhanced by the need to supervise and control the de facto decision-making of the other branches and to check abuses of authority that may arise. The impact of such legislative scrutiny can be profound. It was the congressional investigation of Richard Nixon's role in the Watergate scandal that forced him to resign the presidency, the first such resignation in this nation's history. Bureaucratic abuses also bring down the heavy hand of legislative scrutiny. After the Three Mile Island debacle—in which a crippled nuclear reactor threatened a meltdown—Congress swiftly stepped in to impose a moratorium on construction of new nuclear facilities and ordered an investigation of the Nuclear Regulatory Commission. This was bold action in view of this nation's dependence on foreign oil and the avowed aims of the incumbent President to speed up the development of nuclear energy. Even the justices of the Supreme Court are not immune from congressional oversight, as the impeachment initiative against the late William O. Douglas indicated.

Congress has recently been taking a more active role in day-to-day management and oversight of the bureaucracy. For example, between 1978 and 1982 it has created fifteen independent inspectors general and charged them with promoting economy and efficiency and preventing fraud and abuse in the executive branch. Hitherto inspectors general had existed, but had reported directly to the agencies and departments they watched, and as creatures of those departments they could be removed at will. At the Agriculture Department, for example, where Orville Freeman had administratively established an inspector general in the early 1960s in response to the Billie Sol Estes scandals, it was abolished summarily by Earl Butz a decade later.

It was only in 1976 that Congress statutorily set up its first inspector general (in the erstwhile Department of Health, Education, and Welfare) and its second in 1977 at the Energy Department. In 1978, Congress voted into law a bill creating inspectors-general offices in some twelve additional departments and agencies, in the hope that this would end business as usual in the executive branch and ensure Congress a greater management role.[18] Statistics compiled by the House Select Committee on Committees in 1979 underscore the burgeoning growth in the role of oversight. During the first eleven months of the 96th Congress, the House increased its formal oversight activity by 20 percent over the same period the previous year. More dramatic, compared with the 94th Congress,[19] formal oversight activity was up 50 percent, revealing an important trend. Nevertheless, important as such activities are, Theodore Lowi cautions us not to confuse legislative oversight, a form of committee privilege, with lawmaking.[20]

Another important function of Congress is an outgrowth of big government and an expanding bureaucracy. Plans to dismember the bureaucracy have not fared well in the past. Richard Nixon's proposal to leave only four existing departments intact and to replace the remainder with four others fared poorly. Jimmy Carter, who assumed office promising to cut bureaucratic growth, left office with two additional departments: Energy and Education. It will require tremendous efforts from future presidents to cut back existing departments and agencies even if they succeed in preventing their growth.

Morris Fiorina observed that bureaucratic growth and governmental regulation have caused individuals to call increasingly on congresspeople to act as intermediaries between constituents and government agencies whenever problems arise. Fiorina elaborates: "As the federal role has expanded, Congressmen have shifted emphasis from the controversial (taking positions on issues) to the non-controversial (providing individual favors, etc.)."[21] Increasingly, he claims, they are perceived as ombudsmen serving constituency needs rather than as national policymakers. This whirlwind of activity leaves little time or energy for sponsorship and enactment of new policy. Jack Walker found: "With so many duties and responsibilities thrust upon them it is not surprising that most Senators spend little time in promoting legislative change."[22] Representatives, with the additional burden of seeking reelection every two years, are even more circumscribed.

Meanwhile the President, though still playing a major role in the setting of policy priorities and an agenda for the nation, is not necessarily a beneficiary of congressional deadlock and inaction as far as policy-making is concerned. Indeed, he is its major victim. Even with the aid of the congressional liaison office set up to provide the President with a mechanism for affecting the legislative process, if the legislative success rates of presidents could be assigned grades, the highest average score (69 percent), achieved by Lyndon Johnson, would rate a C. Since only about half the presidential proposals have been passed, a more normal grade would be an F—dismal by any measure.[23] Even when presidential initiatives are passed by Congress, they frequently do not emerge in the form originally presented. Little wonder, then, that especially in the more intractable matters of domestic policy, presidents tend to set forth broad, even grandiose, plans—symbolic initiatives as it were—and then abandon them to the vagaries of congressional whim. Despite the rhetoric of change, the subsequent dismemberment of the Great Society, the New Frontier, and the New American Revolution exemplify this trend. Presidential "honeymoons" may occasionally mask this reality during the first months in office, especially if a president is adept at manipulating public opinion and subtly twisting congressional arms. For example, Ronald Reagan, within his first few months in office, obtained from Congress the tax and spending cuts he requested more or less in the form in which they had been presented. He even managed to obtain strict party-line voting from congressional Republicans. Nevertheless, Congress's tendency to upset the presidential applecart was very much in evidence in the treatment accorded Reagan's proposal to give federal aid in the form of block grants to states for them to disburse, rather than in the form of the hundreds of rigidly defined categorical grants that now exist. According to the National Conference of State Legislatures, although the President's budget proposals in 1981 consolidated 19 percent of existing categorical programs into block grants, the Senate reduced it to 13 percent and the House to 11 percent. Moreover, it was the Republican majority on the Senate Labor and Human Services subcommittee who were instrumental in winning exemptions for various social programs. In the final version of the bill, such major categorical aid items as family planning, community health centers, and most mental health programs were preserved, with the largest program excluded—aid to disadvantaged youngsters, funded at $3.5 billion for fiscal year 1981. Moreover, an opening wedge for the effective vitiation of the block grant concept was contained in Title XVI of the Gramm-Latta bill, which stated that states receiving this money must continue funding "all existing effective programs which are servicing demonstrated needs."[24]

In view of the tendency of Congress to dismember presidential initiatives, presidents have tended eventually to concentrate on foreign policy and the management of day-to-day crises in which congressional cooperation is more likely to be obtained. This means that, especially in matters of domestic public policy, less and less is being accomplished. In any case, the presidential role, like that of Congress, is undergoing redefinition. In his management of day-to-day crises, as in the management of the progress of his legislative initiatives, the President is increasingly being judged not in substantive terms but in symbolic terms. Thomas Cronin has observed that we want our presidents "to serve as teachers, as moral leaders, and occasionally, as folk heroes, as symbolic leaders summoning us as a society to higher achievements. In this role of political leader and teacher, a President develops and sustains the nation's sense of purpose and attempts to reaffirm the nation's credibility and legitimacy."[25]

In the performance of presidential duties, the President is expected to display intangible qualities like "leadership" and "moral tone" and to convey a sense of "reassurance" to the American people. All too often his tangible performance (or lack thereof) is ignored—provided he can inspire public confidence. The overnight transformation of Jimmy Carter's popular standing in the polls after he was perceived to have "taken charge" of the Iranian crisis and the Soviet invasion of Afghanistan in late 1979, or John Kennedy's similar spectacular rise in the ratings following his televised announcement of culpability in the Bay of Pigs fiasco, bear out the public's tendency to respond positively to symbolic rather than substantive performance, especially in matters of foreign policy, and to ignore the lack of progress on the domestic policy front.

The Expanding Roles of the Bureaucracy and the Courts

In any case, the centrifugal forces tugging at Congress, the structural constraints impeding the passage of legislation, and the virtual abdication by recent presidents over the enactment of public policy (especially in the domestic sphere) have created a vacuum of political leadership into which the "unofficial" decision-makers—the bureaucracy and the courts—have stepped. Of necessity, if not by default, they have established a partnership with the elected branches in the making of allocative decisions.

This partnership (some might claim precedence) in policy-making by the nonelected branches has in fact been permitted, perhaps even encouraged, by Congress. In areas where Congress lacks the will to act authoritatively because it perceives the political risks to be unacceptable, it has either drafted vague legislation and left the courts to intercede, or done nothing to alter the status quo, letting the courts intervene first. Some observers go so far as to maintain that "the very idea sometimes is to [let the Courts] handle a problem unsatisfactorily resolved by another branch of government. In areas far from traditional development by case law, indeed in areas often covered densely by statutes and regulations, the Courts have seized the initiative in law making."[26] And in areas where Congress lacks the expertise, the information, or the continuity in office to fulfill its obligations, it has simply delegated its responsibilities to the bureaucracy, leaving agencies to set standards and promulgate rules. This development has not gone unnoticed. One observer even suggested that "the outstanding legal development in this century has been the growth of government policy made by numerous administrative agencies."[27] These prefatory comments concerning the shift in policy-making authority leave us in a better position to consider the expanded role of the courts and the bureaucracy in greater detail.

It should be emphasized at the outset that, like the elected branches, the policy responses of the courts and the bureaucracy are fragmented and ad hoc, determined solely by the immediate pressures they face. Nevertheless, it is precisely the absence of any commitment to a program and the responsiveness of these branches to political pressures that create myriad opportunities for citizens to press their demands for instrumental action. Thus even while electoral linkages have withered, these alternative channels have grown in decision-making importance.

The Political Role of the Bureaucracy

The size of the *Federal Register* (which documents the rules made by agencies) reflects the growing role of the bureaucracy—it has expanded from 20,072 pages in 1968 to 61,261 pages in 1978, a threefold increase in a single decade.[28] Even the scourge of inflation only doubled in the same period. Commenting on this development, Peter Woll has observed that "the volume of such administrative legislation during any given period almost certainly equals the volume of Congressional law making. *The significance of such administrative legislation may also often exceed that of Congress.*"[29]

The recent movement toward deregulation will not necessarily curtail the burgeoning bureaucratic role in policy-making. For one thing, deregulation in one area will not necessarily mean deregulation in others. George Greanias and Duane Windsor provide a particularly insightful analysis on this point.[30] For instance, they have pointed out that elimination of the Civil Aeronautics Board due to the Airlines Deregulation Act (1977) will not add up to less total governmental regulation of the airlines industry. The National Labor Relations Board still deals with labor-management relations; the Federal Aviation Administration still has primary responsibility for traffic safety; the National Transportation Safety Board still investigates air crashes; the Environmental Protection Agency still keeps a watchful eye on air and noise pollution; and the Equal Employment Opportunity Commission still sets requirements for the hiring of women and minorities. Moreover, the Securities and Exchange Commission still affects the industry through securities laws and the accounting provisions of the Federal Corrupt Practices Act, while the Antitrust Division of the Justice Department continues to monitor merger activity.

In theory, bureaucrats are not empowered to legislate. Indeed, it was constitutionally ordained that primary legislative power belonged to the elected branches, principally to Congress. Nevertheless, most observers of the public administration process agree that strict adherence to constitutional theory only serves to obscure the actual role of administrative officials who in practice now share both in the evolution and in the implementation of public policy.

When public policy is being formulated, bureaucrats provide the technical expertise that legislators and executives lack. More important, perhaps, they control the flow of information to decision-makers, which gives them the ability to exercise considerable influence over outcomes. For example, bureaucrats are in a position to report only those facts that fit the stand they favor, or those facts that would lead to a choice of an option their agency or department has the resources to undertake. Such information is often self-serving, intended to buttress the agency's power. The options presented to neophyte President John Kennedy which led him into the Bay of Pigs fiasco exemplify the degree of bureaucratic control over policy choices. In retrospect, Theodore Sorensen blamed "bureaucratic momentum" for the fateful decision to invade Cuba.[31]

Even after policy has been made and emerges in the form of statutory law, new "policies" are continuously evolving in the process of implementation. This tendency has been exacerbated because Congress has in recent years deliberately delegated much of its authority over political decisions to the bureaucracy, either by empowering agencies to set their own rules, but without providing clear guidelines for choice, or by leaving the duties of officials imprecise and vague.

For example, in 1980 the Equal Employment Opportunity Commission was given authority to set its own guidelines concerning sexual harassment on the job and to apply those guidelines to all federal, state, and local governmental agencies as well as virtually all private employers with over 150 employees. Moreover, the commission is empowered to investigate complaints and to negotiate with employers regarding awards for back pay and other kinds of relief. In addition, if the employer refuses to settle, the commission can file suit in federal court requesting relief on the client's behalf. Consider also the Federal Communications Commission. Congress gave it no policy guidelines for licensing stations beyond the criterion of "public convenience, interest, or necessity." Discretionary authority was left entirely to the commission.[32]

The reasons for such complete delegation of authority on the part of Congress are several: legislators are frequently unclear about what they want; it may not be politically expedient for them to say what they do want; or there may be the pressure of time or the need to attend to other legislative tasks. Beyond this, the electoral process itself fails to produce a clear political majority with a definitive mandate. Then too, the lack of coherence in Congress and the absence of a working consensus with the President combine to produce either inaction or imprecise mandates, which permit bureaucrats tremendous discretionary power to interpret, and thus make, law.

Unfortunately the President cannot be counted on to give direction to bureaucrats in departments and agencies nominally under his control. Norton Long has been particularly candid on this point: "A picture of the Presidency as a reservoir from which the lower echelons of administration draw life and vigor is an idealized distortion of reality."[33] Though constitutionally charged with overseeing the implementation and execution of policy, the President, as administrative chief, has few weapons at his command. He can hire only the top echelons, and then only with the advice and consent of the Senate, and he cannot fire most of those under his command. Moreover presidential time and energy are consumed with more pressing matters, among them the development of a legislative program and crisis management. It is career administrative officials who possess the expertise, and they are the ones the interested public contacts.

Most presidents, therefore, though voicing concern over policy implementation, have by and large left it to the agencies and departments to handle on their own. This is especially the case with departments like Housing and Urban Development, Agriculture, and the Interior. Even Franklin Roosevelt, who was fascinated by the administrative process and masterly at manipulating subordinates, conceded failure at controlling the bureaucracy.

Moreover the U.S. Supreme Court has been willing to allow progressively larger delegations of congressional authority to the bureaucracy, despite an initially unfavorable stand in 1935, when in *Schecter Poultry Corporation v. United States* the Court struck down the 1933 National Industrial Recovery Act on the grounds that it was a vague and unconstitutional grant of authority to the executive branch. That act would have permitted industrial groups working through the administrative branch to set prices and production goals. Yet in 1944 the Court reversed itself in *Yakus v. United States* and upheld the Emergency Price Control Act of 1942, which created the Office of Price Administration to administer wage and price controls. Woll claims that during this period the substitution of administrative standards for congressional standards began to be allowed.[34]

Yet on a piecemeal basis and in particular areas, the courts had earlier permitted broad discretionary authority to administrative agencies to regulate prices and control conditions for business. For instance, Civil Aeronautics Board, set up in 1938, was empowered to set air fares and to deny or permit air routes. Subsequently, the Court accepted such vague standards as "just and reasonable," "public interest," "public convenience," and even "excessive profits."[35]

Even without explicit delegations of legislative authority, administrative agencies still make policy. They do so in the process of implementation and adjudication. In the course of implementation the choices made by bureaucrats in meeting their own standards are necessarily political in the sense that they involve and affect allocations or denials of resources. For example, regulatory decisions involving the auto industry, while apparently technical (e.g., the setting of mileage and auto emissions standards), have political effects that ultimately affect production choices and employment. In the case of mileage standards, automakers have had to radically downsize vehicle models, which in turn has made the V-8 engine virtually obsolete, causing the closing of many such engine plants and forcing massive layoffs.

Agencies can also interpret quite broadly their congressional mandate, fashioning its intent to conform with subsequent political mores. For instance, in the Internal Revenue Code of 1954, Congress approved a plan by which taxpayers could take a deduction for contributions to certain tax-exempt organizations, such as those operated exclusively for religious, scientific, charitable, or educational purposes. In 1971 the Internal Revenue Service (IRS) proposed a regulation that would deny deductibility status for private educational institutions that failed to meet certain requirements with respect to eliminating racial discrimination. A U.S. Supreme Court ruling in May 1983 upheld the IRS. By amending or adding to the Internal Revenue

Code so as to facilitate the elimination of racially segregated schools in the South, it should be noted that the agency acted without statutory guidance from Congress and has accomplished something Congress (and state governments) have been unable or unwilling to bring about through legislation.[36]

Adjudicative rulings also can have widespread repercussions. Administrative agencies are not merely charged with writing the regulations but also have the power to fine businesses and persons who are violating those regulations. Some of these rulings may have staggering economic consequences. For example, after the banning of cyclamates by the Food and Drug Administration (FDA) in 1969, Abbott Laboratories, the patent-holder, four years later sought permission from the FDA to resume marketing the sugar substitute. Their bid to do so was rejected by the FDA and by an administrative law judge, resulting in enormous financial losses for the drug company. Another example is the Environmental Protection Agency, which can prohibit the sale of new cars or engines not in compliance with its auto emission standards, prohibit the sale of fuel if it produces emissions that would endanger public health, and impose civil penalties of $10,000 per day for persons found not to be in compliance. Moreover, the Occupational Safety and Health Administration (OSHA), set up in 1971, was empowered to set and enforce safety standards for industry. In its first year alone, 75 percent of some 29,255 workplaces that were inspected were found to be in violation of health and safety standards. OSHA imposed penalties on 45 percent of those establishments.[37]

As a result of bureaucratic decisions, Congress all too often is placed in the position of responding to bureaucratic initiatives. The FDA ban on saccharin is a case in point. When the agency moved to outlaw the artificial sweetener, the angry public response from the public and the food industry prompted Congress to legislate ex post facto a moratorium on (and then a law amending) the proposed FDA ban.[38]

The Political Role of the Supreme Court

That the U.S. Supreme Court has a political role should come as no surprise. Very early on, the Court, under the aggressive leadership of Chief Justice John Marshall, seized the initiative in reviewing acts of Congress in order to determine their constitutionality. Such actions cast doubt on legislative supremacy as it existed, for example, in England, causing one observer to claim that the Supreme Court has always been "continuously, consistently and intimately involved in the policy-making processes of government."[39]

Even so, the Court has lately grown much bolder. While it has seized more opportunities to make policy through declarations of unconstitutionality, it interjects itself to a far greater extent through the process of statutory construction when it reinterprets a law rather than finding it unconstitutional. Such reformulations have become more frequent as the courts are faced with vaguely drafted statutes. In the course of interpretation, however, the courts inevitably make policy. Theodore Lowi's critical observation substantiates this point: "Under present conditions . . . the Court usually ends up rewriting many of the statutes in the course of construction. Since the Court's present procedure is always to find an acceptable meaning for a statute in order to avoid invalidating it, the Court is constantly legislating."[40] Moreover, the scope of the Supreme Court's decisions has become much broader, often extending beyond the individual case to cover basic social issues that Congress has left untouched, issues ranging from abortion and obscenity to medical determinations of life and death. In fact, the courts have been so willing to take on new challenges and tasks that Horowitz maintains, "This has encouraged others to push problems their way, so much so that no Courts anywhere have greater responsibility for making public policy than the Courts of the U.S."[41] In the matter of constitutional interpretation, recent evidence suggests a far more activist bent than in the past. As late as 1957, Robert Dahl in a study of the 167-year history of the Supreme Court found that only seventy-six cases had been struck down, leading him to conclude, "The Court has not effectively substituted its policy goals for those of law-making majorities convened in the elected branches of government."[42] Dahl's earlier findings have, however, been challenged by Jonathan Casper, who in evaluating the Court's role since 1957 finds the judicial activism of the Burger and Warren Courts striking, especially in cases extending the protection of fundamental rights to minorities.[43] In fact, between 1957 and 1978 Casper found that the Court declared thirty-two provisions of federal law unconstitutional in twenty-eight cases. In other words, more than 25 percent of all cases involving a declaration of unconstitutionality have occurred since 1957. Among the cases Casper cites are those involving the rights of aliens (*Trop v. Dallas* [1958] and *Schneider v. Rusk* [1964]), criminal defendants (*United States v. Romans* [1965] and *Leary v. United States* [1969]), war protesters (*Schacht v. United States* [1970]), and poor people (*U.S. Department of Agriculture v. Moreno* [1973]).[44]

One of the most recent instances of judicial willingness to reinterpret congressional action involves the Hyde Amendment (1976), which placed restrictions on Medicaid spending for abortions. In January 1980, New York

District Judge John Dooling struck down the amendment as unconstitutional and ordered the federal government to pay for medically necessary abortions for poor women. While the U.S. Supreme Court justices ultimately upheld the constitutionality of the Hyde Amendment later in the year, their initial refusal to overrule the district court's ruling in the interim led some observers, including Hyde himself, to interpret the Supreme Court's initial actions as a usurpation of congressional power to set spending priorities.[45]

The U.S. Supreme Court has also been involved in statutory reinterpretation, which is ignored by Dahl but stressed by more recent observers, such as Funston, Schubert, Casper, and Lowi. As we have already noted, the Court is increasingly called on to interpret the meaning of federal statutes frequently left deliberately vague by Congress. Glendon Schubert maintains that in the majority of such cases the Court will reformulate the statute under attack in order to avoid ruling it unconstitutional.[46] Casper has conveniently cataloged some of the most recent instances of statutory reinterpretation: the extension of conscientious objector status to those without formal religious training (e.g., *Welsh v. United States* [1970]); restrictions on the use of delinquency provisions against opponents of the Vietnam war (*Breen v. Selective Service Board* [1970]); restrictions on residency requirements for welfare recipients (*Shapiro v. Thompson* [1969]); rulings involving limitations on the power to use surveillance techniques without a warrant (*United States v. U.S. District Court* [1972]).[47]

In cases involving constitutional issues arising in state and local cases (and on which Congress has not spoken), Supreme Court interpretations have affected national policy. For example, Casper cites the area of reapportionment, in which the line of decisions beginning with *Baker v. Carr* (1962) and proceeding through *Reynolds v. Sims* (1964) and on to the later decisions in *Mahan v. Howell* (1973) and *Gaffrey v. Cummings* (1973) produced significant, if piecemeal, changes in districting throughout the nation. Moreover, in almost all such cases, the Court has not been substantially reversed by the passage of subsequent legislation or by constitutional amendment.[48]

The increasingly prominent role of the judiciary will not be easily arrested. Even though the Court's activism of the most recent decades may have grown out of the judicial activism of its members, as Greanias and Windsor argue,[49] the courts will in the future be "impelled regardless of their predilections to adopt a keystone decision-making function in the general processes of government."

Two trends in particular will force an activist role on the judiciary. First, as the general level of governmental activity and, more particularly, administrative activity increases, interested parties will be tempted to seek judicial redress, especially in cases where the administrative penalties imposed are costly or where administrative decisions seem to unfairly favor one constituency over another, with costly consequences for the aggrieved party or advantages for their competitors. For example, when the Depository Institutions Deregulation Committee (DIDC) issued a ruling in August 1981 removing the cap on deposit accounts maturing in four years or more, many banks planned to issue new floating-rate certificates without any limit on the interest rate paid depositors who bought them. However, the U.S. League of Savings Associations promptly brought suit in federal court to stop banks from issuing the new certificates on the grounds that the DIDC had acted illegally by violating the provisions of a 1975 law that permitted thrift institutions to pay a quarter of a percent more in interest than banks do on such certificates. The federal judge ruled that the DIDC had acted illegally. Thus, through a judicial remedy the savings and loan industry was able to preserve its competitive advantage over banks, despite an administrative ruling to the contrary.[50]

Second, as administrative rule-making activity becomes increasingly fractionalized, the courts will continue to be called in to mediate between administrative units themselves. In some cases the courts have already been prevailed on to make policy decisions from among conflicting choices presented to them by two or more agencies with overlapping jurisdictions but conflicting interests. Administrative conflict may even spread to federal-state governments in cases where congressional acts require the states to enforce federal programs and politics. This has been the case particularly with the Environmental Protection Agency (EPA), whose mandate to protect the environment frequently brings it into conflict with other agencies, both state and federal. The ongoing conflict with Ohio over the use of high sulfur coal which required judicial intervention is a case in point.[51]

Under the Clean Air Act of 1970 the EPA had been given responsibility for setting air pollution standards, although the states had the primary task of enforcing those regulations. The use of such coal by Ohio's utility companies produced sulfur-dioxide emissions, with repercussions for acid rain and other undesirable environmental side effects. Various attempts by Governor James Rhodes of Ohio to set implementation standards, beginning in 1972, faced legal challenges by the utility companies, and by 1975, when it became clear that the state had failed to develop a program for sulfur-dioxide emission controls, the federal EPA took the initiative and came forward with its own plan in August 1976. That plan was also challenged in the courts by utility and industrial concerns, and so, by 1977, Governor Rhodes sought to circumvent the EPA by seeking presidential approval to convert Ohio's utilities from natural gas to coal, simultaneously requesting a relaxation of sulfur-dioxide standards until a "practical technology" could be found. The EPA, for its part, took Ohio to court, with the Sixth Circuit Court ruling in the EPA's favor in May 1977. Since then conflict between the state and the EPA has been focused on questions of technology to be used in implementing the air pollution standards set by the EPA. This was one of many instances where the courts have been called on to resolve administrative conflict, and the future portends an increase, rather than a decrease, of similar judicial interventions.

The Changing Means of Popular Influence and Control

In both the initiation and the enactment of public policy, the elected branches have been joined in discharging their responsibilities by the non-elected branches: the courts and the bureaucracy. And these developments have not gone unrecognized by citizens, particularly those of the middle-class majority who possess the resources—the time, money, and technical competence—to address their instrumental actions at those participatory channels that are more likely than voting to yield tangible benefits.

For example, data from various sources confirms that citizens are now more aware of participatory activities other than voting. Consider the trend of responses between 1966 and 1976 to the question posed by the Survey Research Center at the University of Michigan: "Voting is the only way that people like me can have a say about how the government runs things." Table 5 shows that 53 percent of respondents in the sample *disagreed* with the statement, compared with the only 30 percent who had disagreed a decade earlier.

There has been an increase in direct "contacting" types of activities by individuals, including letter-writing (see Figure 2) as well as participation in more organized forms of activity through interest groups. And a majority of those who engage in such activities as letter-writing profess to have found them successful (63 percent) while 77 percent claimed that their efforts to work through organizations were worthwhile (see Tables 6 and 7).

Citizens are also more inclined to go to court. Between 1960 and 1976 the number of civil suits filed in federal district courts more than doubled (see Figure 3).

Table 5

Responses to Question on Extra-electoral Participation, 1966 and 1976

"Voting is the only way that people like me can have a say about how the government runs things."

	1966[a]	1976[b]	Change
Strongly agree Agree	58%	43%	(−15%)
Disagree Strongly disagree	30%	53%	(+23%)
Neutral	10%	2%	
Don't know	2%	2%	

Sources: 1966 Wisconsin data from Jack Dennis, "Support for the Institution of Elections by the Mass Public," *American Political Science Review* 64 (1970): 829. The 1976 data are from *American National Election Study Series, 1976.*
[a] $N = 607$
[b] $N = 3,004$

It is important to note that such participatory acts outside the electoral process are engaged in rationally. Sidney Verba and Norman Nie confirm this point:

Most of the debate on the citizen as rational actor has dealt with him in his role as voter. And voters in general do not measure up to the standards of rationality.... But voting is only one mode of activity. These data on the relative lack of instrumental orientation towards the vote *contrast sharply* with our data on citizen-initiated contacts.[52]

These developments appear to contradict long-standing criticisms that nonelectoral forms of participation are unavoidably and necessarily limited to a few wealthy and organized special interests, which results in the subversion of democracy since the welfare of the larger public (especially of consumers) is left unattended. This position has been articulated by Grant McConnell: "A substantial part of government in the U.S. has come under the influence or control of narrowly based and largely autonomous elites."[53] Andrew Hacker calls these elites "elephants" who by entering the pluralist

Figure 2

Letter-Writing to Public Officials, 1964–1981

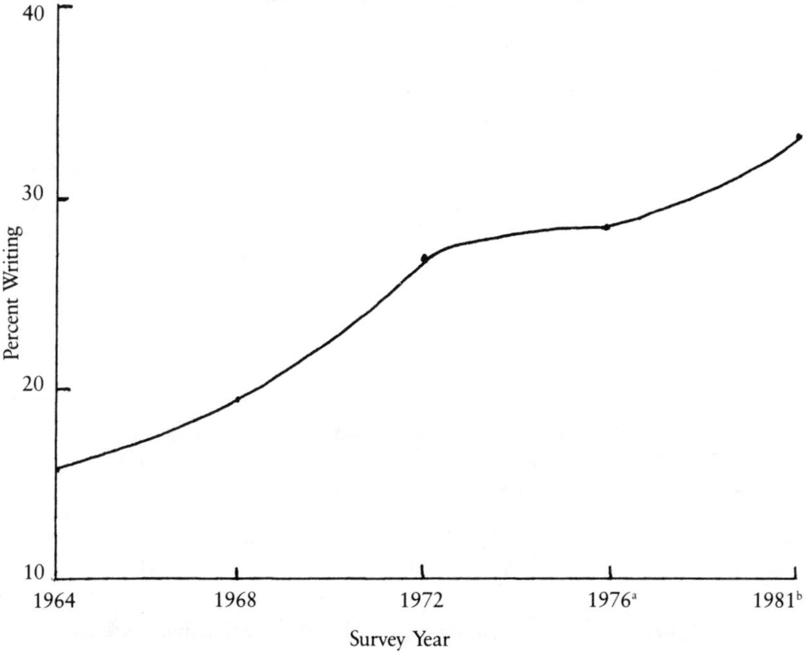

Note: The survey item reads: "Have you ever written any public officials giving them your opinion about something that should be done?"
Source: Codebooks for the year indicated, *American National Election Study Series*, Institute for Social Research, University of Michigan.

[a]*Source:* Adapted from Richard A. Brody, "The Puzzle of Participation," in *The New American Political System*, ed. Anthony King (Washington, D.C.: American Enterprise Institute, 1978), p. 317. By permission of The American Enterprise Institute.
[b]*Source:* Data from author's New Jersey survey. (N.B.: Not statistically comparable; data presented for illustrative purposes only.)

Table 6

Success of Efforts to Contact Local Officials, 1976

		1976[a]
Q: Would you say that speaking or writing to a local leader was generally successful or not successful?	Successful	63%
	Not successful	25%
	Don't know	12%

Source: 1976 data from *American National Election Study Series,* 1976.
[a] N = 543

Table 7

Success of Efforts Through Joining Organizations, 1976

		1976[a]
Q: Would you say that working with others or joining an organization was generally successful or not successful?	Successful	77%
	Not successful	18%
	Don't know	3%
	No answer	2%

Source: 1976 data from *American National Election Study Series,* 1976.
[a] N = 607

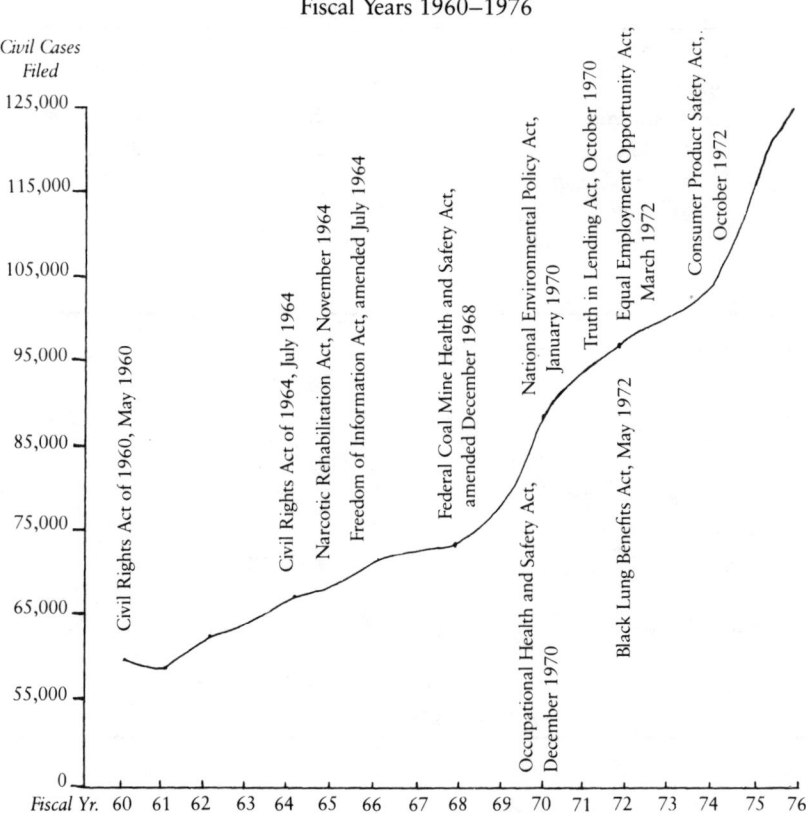

Figure 3

Civil Suits Filed in U.S. District Courts
Fiscal Years 1960–1976

Source: U.S. Government, *Report of the Administrative Office of the Courts of the United States* (Washington, D.C.: Government Printing Office, 1977), p. 120.

arena alongside the "chickens" eliminate public values from effective consideration.[54] Henry Kariel has maintained that at the administrative level of penetration "it is now beyond doubt that the Independent Commission tends to be far from independent; indeed it could not be sovereign even if it ingenuously made the effort. . . . It is ill equipped to consider the objectives of groups outside the calm preserve which it administers jointly with its clientele."[55] Other observers, notably Theodore Lowi, E. E. Schattschneider,

Extra-Electoral Participatory Activity

and Gerald Pomper, have expressed similar concerns, Pomper in particular being fearful that the breakdown of the electoral process due to party decline will mean a loss of popular influence over public policies.[56] It is our view that the fears of pluralist critics are greatly exaggerated. Nonelectoral participation in the United States today is not the sole preserve of the few; it is far more broad-based. This will become clear when we examine the changed means of popular influence and popular control in greater detail.

Popular Influence at the Administrative Level

The recognition that public policy is not made through the electoral process is so widespread that it has spawned something new: a host of public interest pressure groups. Jeffrey Berry estimates that almost half (47 percent) of the groups he examined in 1973 were formed between 1968 and 1973.[57] Their entry onto the political scene in competition with private interests may be one of the most striking developments of the 1970s. As one observer points out, such groups "now supplement the void in the array of forces represented in the traditional pluralistic bargaining process" by representing the "very broad, diffuse, non-commercial interests which [previously] received little direct representation" in the processes by which policy is made.[58]

There are various estimates of the number of such public interest groups and the people who belong to them. In 1977, Berry estimated that public interest groups represent some 3 million people, but more recent estimates put their numbers much higher.[59] In a 1979 study of fifteen national environmental groups alone, Robert Camaron Mitchell of "Resources for the Future" estimated their combined membership at over 2 million.[60] Common Cause and Ralph Nader's Public Citizen Inc. are estimated to have 225,000 and 80,000 members respectively. Over the past few years, such groups have proliferated and grown in membership, among them the National Trust for Historic Preservation, with 160,000 members in 1980 (vs. 35,000 in 1974); the National Abortion Rights Action League, with 90,000 members (vs. 35,000 to 40,000 in 1977); and Handgun Control Inc., with 80,000 members (vs. 200 in 1975). The Office of Neighborhoods, Voluntary Associations, and Consumer Affairs of the U.S. Department of Housing and Urban Development has identified over 15,000 consumer and citizen groups.[61]

The involvement of citizens has been mandated by Congress. The first federal requirements for citizen participation were established in the Administrative Procedures Act of 1946. The trend toward including public participation then accelerated in the 1960s, especially at the local level, when citizen involvement was mandated by various federal categorical grant programs such as Urban Renewal and Model Cities, which were designed to ensure "maximum feasible participation." Despite the unhappy experiences with these early attempts to include the public,[62] the trend has continued even after revenue-sharing replaced many of those grants. For example, the Housing and Community Development Act of 1974 and the State and Local Assistance Act of 1972 required citizen participation under the Community Development Block Grant Program.[63] A 1975 study of the Commonwealth of Pennsylvania indicated that more than 165 statutes requiring advisory committees or public hearings had been passed.[64] On the national level, several recent legislative programs require citizen participation, among them the National Environmental Policy Protection Act and the Federal Water Pollution Act.

Groups like these, while initially hobbled financially in comparison with mammoth corporate interests, have been able to convert their political sophistication and technical expertise into developing successful methods of acquiring adequate funding. These range from complex direct mail techniques to obtaining funds from sympathetic foundations. The success of these groups is reflected in the size of their budgets. In 1979, for example, fifteen of the largest environmental groups had a combined budget of $100 million, while Common Cause was able to raise $5.3 million and Nader's Public Citizen Inc. raised $1 million. More recent attempts to undercut the activities of public interest groups, in part by severing the ties between federal grant money and political advocacy or restricting the use of the Freedom of Information Act, have yet to prove lethal to their activities.[65]

Although such groups tend to overrepresent the interests of the middle-class mass public, the "haves," there are no structural impediments to representation of the interests of the have-nots, and in time we may well see the advent of public interest pressure groups oriented toward representing the poor. Some already exist, among them the Community Services Society in New York City and the National Welfare Rights League.

Louis Dexter observes that while public interest pressure groups can and do operate on the congressional level, "there is no reason for most Washington representatives to spend the bulk of their time on legislative lobbying."[66] Indeed, a major focus of public interest pressure group activity has been directed at the courts and the bureaucracy, more particularly at those regulatory agencies that have in the past been the most susceptible to capture by private interests. Jeffrey Berry's 1977 study indicated that 47 percent of his sample named administrative agencies or departments as major or secondary targets for their activities.⁶⁷ The realization that policy is refined and conflicting interests are ultimately resolved in agency proceedings is increasing. This focus on the bureaucracy has also been noted by Edgar Shor, editor of a symposium on the subject conducted in 1977, who describes the contemporary situation:

> By now very few sectors of the national Executive Branch have escaped the probing, prodding, direct intervention or judicial challenge from a variety of organizations which for lack of a generic designation are variously labelled "citizen groups" or "public interest groups." ... To fill the "advocacy gap" resulting from a monopoly of access enjoyed by narrowly focused and well financed private interests, the public advocates have demanded participation in agency proceedings on behalf of diffuse, poorly organized or inarticulate public concerns.⁶⁸

Intrusion at this level does present problems for public interest groups. For one thing, it is often prohibitively costly. Active participation in one FDA rule-making proceeding was estimated in 1972 at $30,000 to $40,000, adjudicatory proceedings being even more expensive.⁶⁹ Moreover, whenever a public interest pressure group does file a statement, it must compete for agency attention with a number of commercial interests who have more data to present and who possess more specialized information. Nevertheless, there have been a few notable victories for public interest pressure groups operating at the agency level. For example, the banning of Red Dye No. 2 by the FDA was the result of a four-year campaign by health research groups, while the termination of most uses of DDT by the EPA was the result of an effort by the Environmental Defense Fund.⁷⁰

Public interest pressure groups promote their causes in other ways. Even if formal interventions are too expensive, informal monitoring of agency decisions has been successful. Such tactics include embarrassment of the agency, especially through the media. The finding of dissident agency researchers on saccharin, though suppressed by the FDA, were publicized through the actions of public interest pressure groups acting through the media. Watchdog activities of this sort have the potential to make agency decision-makers constantly mindful of the public interest.

There is evidence that the activity of public interest pressure groups will become institutionalized. Edgar Shor has indicated progress on several fronts. First, money is being sought from governmental sources to promote representation from groups and individuals lacking effective representation. Congress and federal agencies have begun to respond. Many government agencies have developed experimental programs to reimburse citizen groups for participation in agency proceedings. The Federal Trade Commission, for example, with an authorization of $1 million annually, has spent $2 million on some sixty groups who participated in eighteen rule-making hearings since 1974. Moreover, the 1976 Toxic Substances Control Act gave the EPA power to subsidize consumer groups, while the FDA also began a $250,000 pilot program in 1980. And in response to a petition by Consumers' Union, the Consumer Product Safety Commission agreed in December 1976 to fund such a reimbursement program even without explicit statutory directives to do so. In 1980, for example, the commission awarded $50,000 to consumer groups to reimburse them for the costs of participating in agency proceedings.[71]

Second, some public interest organizations have urged establishment of new governmental entities within the executive branch to provide official advocates of the public interest. Shor notes that as a result several agencies have established in-house units to provide internal advocacy of consumer and other interests. Still to gain congressional approval is a measure that would establish an Agency for Consumer Protection,[72] which would be charged with representing the public interest (that of consumers) before federal agencies and in the courts.

Third, passage of the so-called "Sunshine Law" in September 1976, which required more than fifty agencies and commissions to open their meetings to the public, should provide consumer groups with greater and more permanent direct access to the centers of decision-making.

Popular Influence at the Judicial Level

An equally important recent development reflecting the shift in decision-making to judicial channels as well has been the rise of public interest law firms, among them the Center for Law and Social Policy; the Public Citizen Litigation Group; the Institute for Public Interest Representation at Georgetown University Law School; and the National Resources Defense Council, a leading environmental public interest law firm.[73] There are signs that on this front the have-nots are represented. For example, Public Advocates Inc. of San Francisco describes itself as the "first general interest law firm in the West." Funding for such enterprises has been obtained from various sources. The American Bar Association and several foundations recently funded the Council of Public Interest Law, and the Ford Foundation funded the National Resources Defense Council. There has been a steady increase in the percentage of cases brought by such nonprofit organizations suing to challenge not "some narrow determination of interest to only one party, but the policy as a whole and the assumptions on which it is based."[74] Depending on where they have chosen to file suit, their success rate has been remarkable. Environmentalist groups that have sued in the District of Columbia (using either the U.S. District Court or the U.S. Court of Appeals) have obtained favorable rulings in fifty-eight out of sixty-five cases over the past decade, a 68 percent win ratio.[75]

Public interest litigation has tended to proceed in two ways: The first method is the filing of *amicus curiae* briefs in which a public interest law firm presents the court with information or legal arguments not being presented by the litigants. Although originally intended to be neutral, such briefs have become increasingly partisan. For instance, in 1979 the National Resources Defense Council (NRDC) filed an *amicus* brief challenging the government plan to lease blocks off the Georges Bank (off Massachusetts) for oil and gas exploration.[76] The second method, that of litigation sponsorship or direct law suits, is much more expensive, but public interest law firms have not shied away from taking this road either. For example, an NRDC attorney served as co-counsel jointly with the Wilderness Society in a suit against construction of the Trans-Alaska pipeline.

Although both the Georges Bank and the Alaska pipeline cases were unsuccessfully resolved, the courts have in general encouraged public interest litigation, especially in cases where prior administrative action has been unsuccessful. In particular, broad judicial interpretations of two recent vaguely worded statutes have encouraged public interest litigation—the National Environmental Policy Act of 1969 and the Freedom of Information Act of 1966 (amended in 1974).

The National Environmental Policy Act required an "environmental impact statement" prior to proposals for "any major federal actions significantly affecting the human environment." This opened the door to a host of environmental litigation. For example, a court order obtained by the NRDC successfully and indefinitely delayed a plan by the Bonneville Power Administration (BPA) to build up to thirty coal-fired plants in the Pacific Northwest because the BPA had not finished the required environmental impact statement. In another case, the NRDC obtained from the U.S. Court of Appeals a ruling that the Nuclear Regulatory Commission (NRC) could not license facilities to recover plutonium from spent nuclear fuel until the NRC made a "generic programmatic environmental review." Administration plans for a breeder reactor program were subsequently shelved.[77] The Freedom of Information Act (FIA) has also been used by several public interest groups, particularly by the Ralph Nader organization, as the basis for suits.

Some of the legal doctrines that have been obstacles to public interest litigation (impediments such as legal standing, sovereign immunity, and jurisdiction) have been eroded in the past decade.[78] In addition, the availability of court-awarded counsel fees to successful parties under an amendment to the FIA has been another inducement to public interest litigaton. Even though the legal standards applicable to judicial review still remain highly favorable to the government, "courts today play a more prominent and less interstitial role in defining and protecting the public interest often against agencies accused of neglecting it."[79] Thus, despite the political importance of nonelectoral channels, there is reason to hope that the public interest can still be protected and that popular influence over the direction of public policy will be maintained.

The Changing Means of Popular Control

The citizen-participant model, like the pluralist model, could be attacked as undemocratic on other grounds, chief among them the fear that the nonelected branches, impervious to the electoral sanction, will be uncontrollable and unaccountable for the public decisions they make, unlike elected officials who can be removed from office. It is our position, however, that the unique design of the U.S. Constitution, which incorporated the device of institutional checks and balances, now operates in lieu of elections to hold nonelected officials in check.

For example, bureaucrats are prevented from acting irresponsibly not only by Congress's zealously exercising its oversight role but also by additional mechanisms built into the system which have been expanded in number over the years. Such controls make it possible (1) for administrative agencies to check one another, as when the tax court reviews decisions of the Internal Revenue Service; (2) for the judiciary to review administrative decisions between units and between administrative units and their affected constituencies; and (3) for Congress to exercise oversight primarily through the General Accounting Office. To facilitate public control, public interest groups have exploited these mechanisms. One instance of such interbureaucratic checks is the complaint recently filed with the Federal Trade Commission (FTC) by Public Advocates Inc. on behalf of the American G.I. Forum, I.M.A.G.E. (the largest U.S.-Hispanic government employee group), and the Grey Panthers against the U.S. Secretary of the Treasury and his "agents," including the Secretary of Labor and "substantial numbers of top corporate and government officials," for their roles in promoting the 1979 Savings Bond Drive. Because this promotion minimized the low rates of interest offered, Public Advocates Inc. labels the government's advertising program "the most costly series of deceptive acts engaged in by any corporation or governmental agency in recent history." The complaint was brought under a provision of the FTC statute that bars any "unfair or deceptive act or practice in or affecting commerce." It seeks sweeping quasi-judicial relief, including temporary suspension of all such promotional activity pending publication, through a series of "corrective ads," of the many disadvantages of savings bonds compared with other long-term investments. As yet the FTC has taken no action, but the complaint does exemplify an increasing tendency on the part of public interest groups to resort to and expand on institutional mechanisms of control on behalf of a broader "public" interest.[80]

The overlapping of responsibilities encourages interbureaucratic rivalry. Thus the American political system leaves the informed public with numerous opportunities to offset the administrative decisions of one arm of the bureaucracy with another. While this may not lead to efficient government, it does provide for a considerable degree of public control.

In other situations the courts can be prevailed on to check the bureaucracy. Judicial review of administrative acts began with the Administrative Procedures Act of 1946. By spelling out basic procedural rules for agencies to follow, this act made administrative determinations subject to judicial review. For some time, however, such judicial review could be exercised only on narrow procedural grounds, for instance, if due process standards had been ignored. It was rarely possible to challenge the substantive decisions of administrative agencies.

During the 1970s, however, many obstacles to carrying policy problems to the courts were removed. For instance, Donald Horowitz notes that as requirements for legal standing have changed, "courts have become a more prominent part of the process of administrative decision-making. They have moved beyond protection of the rights of parties aggrieved by administrative action to participation in problem solving. . . . *Judicial review has passed from matters of procedure to matters of both procedure and substance.*"[81] Moreover, although administrative agencies have their own judicial proceedings, Horowitz claims that the courts are beginning to become "less and less hospitable to administrative claims of immunity from judicial oversight."[82]

A case study by Roland Speidel serves to illustrate this point. Speidel investigated the procedure by which disappointed bidders on government contracts could appeal the decision.[83] Formerly, disappointed bidders for government contracts could turn to two administrative channels for review of an unfavorable decision: the procuring agency itself or the General Accounting Office, the protest being lodged with the comptroller-general. Usually both channels upheld the agency decision. For example, in 1971, of seventy-four protests of awards granted, only 5 percent of review decisions recommended cancellations of contracts. Of late, however, disappointed bidders have been turning to the courts for judicial review of adverse administrative decisions. Prior to January 1970, unsuccessful bidders seeking declaratory or injunctive relief had no legal standing to sue and so were unable to obtain judicial review. Under the prevailing rules of standing, plaintiffs had "no right to a government contract which could be invaded by an improper governmental action." Yet in the case of *Scanwell Laboratories v. Shaffer* (1970), an important if inconclusive precedent was set. The court of appeals in this issue used the Administrative Procedures Act to overcome the obstacles of sovereign immunity and legal standing and found for the defendant.

Under other circumstances, the courts can be utilized to alter the substance of policy made by administrative decisions if it can be shown that those decisions had an adverse effect on the public interest. One particular case embroiled the Federal Power Commission (FPC) in a controversy concerning the siting of "Storm King," a 2,000-megawatt hydroelectric facility on the Hudson River forty miles north of New York City. The decision in this case was feared to have been made in the interests of the FPC's well-heeled corporate "client," Con Edison.[84] The FPC's initial approval of this site was vehemently opposed by an environmental public interest group, the Scenic Hudson Preservation Conference. Although successful in obtaining permission to participate at the agency level, Scenic Hudson was unsuccessful at blocking approval for the project at the FPC hearings. Turning therefore to the court, Scenic Hudson was able to mount a continuing challenge to Con Edison's efforts to build its power plant, on the basis that the environmental impact of such a plant had not been sufficiently investigated. In the near future we can expect to see further efforts to challenge the agency-client relationship by public interest groups operating through judicial channels.

Congress may also oversee the bureaucracy through the General Accounting Office (GAO) and the information provided by the Congressional Research Service. Particularly through GAO oversight reports, recommendations may be issued to administrative agencies. A case in point was the report submitted to Congress in 1972 at the request of Congressman John Dingell of Michigan and entitled "Improvements Needed in Federal Efforts to Implement the National Environmental Policy Act." In its report the GAO was critical of the fact that environmental impact statements were not being filed in a timely manner and recommended that public participation be given more emphasis.

Even if the bureaucracy can be held in check, can the courts be controlled? By what means can those judges who are appointed be held accountable? Glendon Schubert has suggested several formal and informal mechanisms by means of which the courts can be held democratically accountable for political decisions.[85] For instance, the U.S. Supreme Court is sensitive to shifts in public opinion and can be persuaded to overrule itself; in fact, it has done so on several occasions. The most dramatic and well-known instance was probably its legal about-face on the matter of racial segregation when *Plessy v. Ferguson* (1896) was reversed some fifty years later by *Brown v. Board of Education of Topeka* (1954). Another important Supreme Court reversal occurred in *Minersville School District v. Gobitis* (1940), a "loyalty" case involving the expulsion of two schoolchildren because they did not salute the American flag as commanded by official regulations. In the subsequent trial their parents, who were Jehovah's Witnesses, claimed that such an act was forbidden by their religion. Justice Felix Frankfurter, writing for the majority of eight, declared a judicial hands-off policy by stating that such a matter was best left for public opinion and its expression in statutory legislation. Yet in 1943 the Court reversed itself and, by a majority of six, overruled the *Gobitis* decision. It now saw the case as involving the rights of the individual versus the authority of the state and therefore doubted whether the state had the right to prescribe such rules or enforce compliance from citizens.[86]

The normal operations of checks and balances can also circumscribe the decision-making powers of the U.S. Supreme Court. Prodded by public opinion, Congress can be persuaded to overrule the Court by passing new legislation if public opposition to an unpopular Court decision is fierce. For instance, the Omnibus Crime Control and Safe Streets Act of 1968 was intended to overrule the effects of some objectionable Court decisions made during the previous decade which appeared to many to strengthen a criminal's civil rights. Three decisions in particular were targeted: *Mallory v. United States* (1957), which held the accused must be arraigned without unnecessary delay; *Miranda v. Arizona* (1966), in which the Court ruled that accused persons must be advised of their rights before interrogation; and *United States v. Wade* (1967), in which the Court ruled that accused persons had the right to counsel when involved in police lineups. Senator John McClellan of Arkansas voiced the opinion of many when he stated that these decisions resulted in the "freeing of multitudes of criminals of undoubted guilt," and this feeling undoubtedly impelled Congress to respond with new legislation designed to strengthen local police forces.[87]

Another example was the response of Congress in 1977 to a 1976 Court ruling that pregnancy did not have to be covered by the health and temporary disability plans of employers. Congress enacted legislation that required employers to include pregnancy, childbirth, and related medical conditions in their health insurance and disability plans.[88]

If public outcry is strong, Congress can always overturn a Supreme Court declaration that an act is unconstitutional by amending the Constitution—or at least threaten to do so. Such public concern followed the 1962 *Engel v. Vitale* decision, which outlawed prayer in New York's public schools. This decision was followed a year later by the *School District of Abington Township v. Schempp* case (1963), which outlawed school prayer throughout the nation. The immediate reaction of Congress was to propose an amendment to the Constitution allowing prayer in school. Following the *Engel* decision, some 75 versions of the amendment were introduced, 22 in the Senate and 53 in the House; some 146 more were introduced after *Schempp*.[89] None of these amendments was successfully passed and in this case the Court's decision was left standing.[90]

The public can choose other more direct means of expressing its opposition to the Supreme Court's determinations. The violent reactions to the Court's rulings on busing or the location of low-income housing in racially segregated neighborhoods are examples. Like the bureaucracy, the Supreme Court, though unelected, is still subject to popular control.

Class Bias in Political Participation and Voting

Not all Americans can or do participate. Despite the pluralism and permeability of the political process, and the relative ease of access to decision-makers, participatory activity through nonelectoral channels is still far more complex than the simple act of voting. While voting requires minimal levels of time, money, and political know-how, participatory activity through extra-electoral channels requires much more.

The "haves" possess the requisite organizational skills, financial resources, political sophistication in greater measure than the "have-nots." Hence it is the haves who have adjusted best to the altered realities of our political process and who are the most capable of addressing their instrumental actions at these channels which count the most. As a result of their efforts, they tend to receive a disproportionate share of the tangible benefits, and this in turn can be expected to make them supportive of the status quo. Conversely, the have-nots (those who are poor or of minority status) and the not-yet-haves (the young) are less likely to be able to function well in the complex political environment. Because these groups therefore obtain relatively fewer benefits from the system, they are more likely to value it less.

Thus, when it comes to practicing such symbolic rituals as voting, the middle-class bias of participatory activity continues to be reflected in the bias of electoral participation.

Notes

1. Joseph Schumpeter, *Capitalism, Socialism, and Democracy* (New York: Harper & Row, 1942), p. 250.
2. Gerald Pomper, *Elections in America: Control and Influence in Democratic Politics* (New York: Dodd, Mead & Co., 1968), p. 149. Emphasis added.
3. Ibid., p. 203.
4. Benjamin Ginsberg, "Elections and Public Policy," *American Political Science Review* 70 (March 1976): 41–49.
5. See Norman C. Thomas and Harold L. Wolman, "The Presidency and Policy Formulation: The Task Force Device," *Public Administration Review* 24 (September/October 1969): 463.
6. See Stephen J. Wayne, *The Legislative President* (New York: Harper & Row, 1978).
7. Kirk H. Porter and Donald B. Johnson, *National Party Platforms, 1840–1968* (Urbana: University of Illinois Press, 1970), p. 756.
8. Quoted in *Congressional Quarterly Almanac 1976*, p. 865.
9. John M. Bacheller, "Lobbyists and the Legislative Process: The Impact of Environmental Constraints," *American Political Science Review* 71 (March 1977): 253–62. (In 1937 the President's Committee on Administrative Management had found that at least two-thirds of all public bills passed by Congress emanated from the administrative branch.)
10. Jack Walker, "Setting the Agenda in the U.S. Senate," *British Journal of Political Science* 7 (October 1977): 445.
11. David Mayhew, *Congress: The Electoral Connection* (New Haven: Yale University Press, 1976), p. 62.
12. *Congressional Quarterly Almanac 1977*, p. 11.
13. Mayhew, *Congress*, p. 99.
14. See George Shipman, "Role of the Administrator—Policymaking as Part of the Administrative Process," in *Policies, Decisions, and Organizations*, ed. Fremont J. Lyden, George Shipman, and Norton Kroll (New York: Appleton-Century-Crofts, 1969), chap. 8. Emphasis added.
15. *Congressional Quarterly Almanac 1965*, p. 66.
16. Barber Conable, quoted in *Barron's*, July 20, 1981, pp. 4–5.

17. Mayhew, *Congress*, pp. 132–34.
18. See *Barron's*, June 16, 1980, p. 4.
19. *Congressional Quarterly Almanac 1979*, p. 15.
20. Theodore Lowi, *The End of Liberalism: The Second Republic of the United States*, 2d ed. (New York: W. W. Norton & Co., 1979), p. 107.
21. Morris Fiorina, "The Case of the Vanishing Marginals: The Bureaucracy Did It," *American Political Science Review* 77 (March 1977): 181. Fiorina's observation has been confirmed in an interview with Stephen Jurash, an intern in one of the district offices of Congressman James Florio of New Jersey. Jurash estimates that 80 percent of the congressman's time is spent on district services and is conducting a management study to determine cost-efficient methods of processing constituency demands.
22. Walker, "Setting the Agenda," p. 424.
23. For legislative success rates, see *Congressional Quarterly Weekly Report*, December 9, 1978, p. 3408.
24. Quoted in an editorial in the *Wall Street Journal*, July 21, 1981, p. 28. Moreover, it has become clear that in spite of Reagan's campaign pledges to reduce federal spending and to shift money from civilian to defense programs, the opposite has occurred. In large part this has been because Reagan's budgets have been overhauled by Congress in the normal course of the budgetary process. The effect of this on federal spending is shown in the table below.

Federal Spending Categories as
a Percentage of the Gross National Product

Year	Total Spending	Transfers to Persons
1976	22.4%	9.2%
1977	22.0%	8.8%
1978	21.3%	8.4%
1979	21.1%	8.5%
1980	22.9%	9.4%
1981	23.4%	9.6%
1982 (I)	24.3%	9.9%
1982 (II)	24.2%	10.1%
1982 (III)	24.9%	10.4%
1982 (IV)	26.3%	10.9%

(*Source*: Survey of Current Business, Economic Report of the President, 1983. Data seasonally adjusted.)

As a percentage of the gross national product, federal spending has thus increased between 1980 and 1982, while "transfers to persons" actually declined for some of the Carter years but increased under Reagan.

25. Quoted in Rexford Tugwell and Thomas Cronin, eds., *The Presidency Reappraised* (New York: Praeger, 1974), p. 236.
26. Donald Horowitz, *The Courts and Social Policy* (Washington, D.C.: The Brookings Institution, 1977), p. 5. One caveat to bear in mind when assessing the U.S. Supreme Court's policy-making role is that the Court does not initiate its agenda—cases must be brought to the Court.
27. William Boyer, *Bureaucracy on Trial: Policy-making by Governmental Agencies* (New York: Bobbs-Merrill Co., 1964), p. 2.
28. Quoted in the *Wall Street Journal*, May 23, 1979, p. 26.
29. Peter Woll, *American Bureaucracy*, 2d ed. (New York: W. W. Norton & Co., 1977), p. 12. Emphasis added.
30. George Greanias and Duane Windsor, "The Courts: The New Keystone Decision-makers," Paper presented at the Southern Political Science Association Meeting, November 1980, p. 8.
31. Quoted in John C. Donovan, *The Policy Makers* (New York: Pegasus Press, 1970), p. 32.
32. For an extended discussion on this point, see Louis Mainzer's *Political Bureaucracy* (Glenville, Ill.: Scott, Foresman & Co., 1973), p. 40n.
33. Norton Long, "Power and Administration," in *Bureaucratic Power in National Politics*, ed. Francis E. Rourke, 3d ed. (Boston: Little, Brown & Co., 1978) p. 8.
34. Woll, *American Bureaucracy*, p. 163. The Emergency Price Control Act of 1942 had created an Office of Price Administration to administer wage and price controls. The U.S. Supreme Court upheld this delegation of authority in the case of *Yakus v. United States* (1944).
35. Mainzer, *Political Bureaucracy*, p. 40.
36. See James Kilpatrick in *The Toledo Blade*, August 10, 1979, p. 8. Certain congresspeople had moved to suspend enforcement of the IRS rule pending congressional review. In a 1983 ruling, the Court upheld the IRS in a case brought by Bob Jones University, the affected party.
37. *Congressional Quarterly Almanac 1970*, p. 474.
38. *Wall Street Journal*, May 23, 1979, p. 18.
39. Richard Funston, "Supreme Court and Critical Elections," *American Political Science Review* 69 (September 1975): 795.
40. Lowi, *The End of Liberalism*, p. 300.
41. Horowitz, *The Courts and Social Policy*, p. 3.
42. See Robert Dahl, "Decision-making in a Democracy: The Role of the Supreme Court in National Policy-making," *Journal of Public Law* 6 (Fall 1957): 279–95. Somewhat similarly, William Landes and R. A. Posner see the Court as the enforcer of past deals made by effective interest groups with earlier legislatures.

See "The Independent Judiciary in an Interest Group Perspective," *Journal of Law and Economics* 18 (December 1975): 875–911.
43. Jonathan Casper, "The Supreme Court and National Policy-making," *American Political Science Review* 70 (March 1976): 56.
44. Ibid., pp. 52–54.
45. Quoted in the *Cleveland Plain Dealer*, February 20, 1980, p. 1.
46. See Glendon Schubert, *Constitutional Politics: The Political Behavior of Supreme Court Justices and the Constitutional Policies That They Make* (New York: Holt, Rinehart & Winston, 1960), p. 175.
47. See Casper, "The Supreme Court and National Policy-making," p. 57.
48. See Ibid., p. 58.
49. Greanias and Windsor, "The Courts," p. 11.
50. See *Wall Street Journal*, August 3, 1981, p. 30.
51. For an extended discussion of this problem, see Ervin Shienbaum, "Intergovernmental Efforts to Achieve Energy Policies: An Examination of Administrative Dynamics Regarding Ohio's High Sulfur Coal Question," Report prepared for the Ohio Interuniversity Energy Research Council, 1980.
52. Sidney Verba and Norman Nie, *Participation in America: Political Democracy and Social Equality* (New York: Harper & Row, 1972), p. 104.
53. Grant McConnell, *Private Power and American Democracy* (New York: Alfred A. Knopf, 1966), p. 339.
54. Andrew Hacker, *The End of the American Era* (New York: Atheneum Press, 1970), p. 42.
55. Henry Kariel, *The Decline of American Pluralism* (Stanford, Calif.: Stanford University Press, 1961), p. 89. These views have been challenged by two recent works. See Paul J. Quirk, *Industry Influence in Federal Regulatory Agencies* (Princeton: Princeton University Press, 1981), and Thomas R. Dunlap, *D.D.T.: Citizens, Scientists and Public Policy* (Princeton: Princeton University Press, 1981).
56. Gerald Pomper, "Decline of the Party in Elections," *Political Science Quarterly* 92 (Spring 1977): 41. See also E. E. Schattschneider, *The Semi-Sovereign People* (New York: Holt, Rinehart & Winston, 1960) and Theodore Lowi, *The End of Liberalism* , 2d ed. (New York: W. W. Norton & Co., 1969; 2d ed., 1979).
57. Jeffrey Berry, *Lobbying for the People* (Princeton: Princeton University Press, 1977), p. 34.
58. Peter Shuck, "Public Interest Groups and the Policy Process," *Public Administration Review*, March/April 1977, p. 133. See also Jeffrey M. Berry, *Lobbying for the People*.
59. Berry, *Lobbying for the People*, p. 134.
60. See the *National Journal*, July 12, 1980, p. 1136.

61. See Stuart Langton, *Citizen Participation in America* (Lexington, Mass.: Lexington Books, 1978), p. 2.
62. See especially Daniel Patrick Moynihan, *Maximum Feasible Misunderstanding* (New York: The Free Press, 1969).
63. See Joseph Lee Rodgers, Jr., *Citizen Committees* (Cambridge, Mass.: Ballinger Publishing Co., 1977), and John D. Hutcheson, Jr., and Jan Shevin, *Citizen Groups in Local Politics* (Santa Barbara, Calif.: American Bibliographical Center–Clio Press, 1976).
64. Langton, *Citizen Participation*, p. 5.
65. *National Journal*, July 12, 1980, p. 1136. In 1983 the Office of Management and Budget, for example, proposed revisions to federal purchasing rules which would prevent federal money from being used to pay the salaries, office rents, or equipment of organizations whose primary purpose is political advocacy. Public interest groups, among others, have contended that the revisions would violate their First Amendment rights to freedom of expression and are preparing lawsuits to challenge the revisions on those grounds. (*National Journal*, February 19, 1983, p. 371.)
66. Louis Anthony Dexter, *How Organizations are Represented in Washington* (Indianapolis: Bobbs-Merrill Co., 1969), p. 7.
67. Berry, *Lobbying for the People*, p. 56.
68. Edgar Shor, ed., "Public Interest Representation in the 1980s," *Public Administration Review*, March/April 1977, p. 131.
69. Shuck, "Public Interest Groups," p. 155.
70. Ibid.
71. *National Journal*, May 10, 1980, p. 778.
72. Shor, "Public Interest Representation," p. 132.
73. Public interest groups are not necessarily liberal. Two conservative groups which have championed the cause of big business are the Mountain States Legal Foundation and the Pacific Legal Foundation.
74. Donald Horowitz, "The Courts as Guardians of the Public Interest," *Public Administration Review*, March/April 1977, p. 150.
75. This compares, however, with a 41 percent win ratio for cases litigated elsewhere. *National Journal*, December 19, 1981, p. 2234.
76. *Wall Street Journal*, February 20, 1980, p. 18.
77. Ibid.
78. See Karren Orren, "Standing to Sue: Interest Group Conflict Before the Courts," *American Political Science Review* 70 (September 1976): 723–41.
79. Horowitz, "The Courts as Guardians," p. 150n.
80. Example from Robert M. Bleiberg in *Barron's*, February 11, 1980, p. 7.

81. Horowitz, "The Courts as Guardians," p. 150n. Emphasis added.
82. Ibid., p. 155.
83. Roland Speidel, "Judicial and Administrative Review of Government Contract Awards," *Law and Contemporary Problems* 37 (Winter 1972): 63–94.
84. See Ervin Shienbaum, "Interorganizational Dynamics of Electric Power Siting (Ph.D. diss., New York University, 1979), chap. 6.
85. Schubert, *Constitutional Politics*, p. 263.
86. See Morris L. Ernst, *The Great Reversals* (New York: Weybright & Talley, 1973), p. 137.
87. See Adam Carlyle Breckinridge, *Congress Versus the Court* (Lincoln: University of Nebraska Press, 1970), p. 4.
88. See *Congressional Quarterly Almanac 1978*, p. 22.
89. See Theodore Becker, ed., *The Impact of Supreme Court Decisions* (New York: Oxford University Press, 1969), pp. 23–27.
90. *Congressional Quarterly Almanac 1972*, p. 496. Arguing along the same lines, Richard Neely maintains that the Courts make American democracy work by doing what the other branches are incapable of doing. See *How Courts Govern America* (New Haven, Conn.: Yale University Press, 1981).

FOUR

THE SYMBOLISM OF ELECTIONS AND THE RITUALISM OF VOTING

We now turn to the first of the two decisions involved in voting, whether to go to the polls at all. In the American context, this is the more important decision. The second decision is an act generally acknowledged to be performed noninstrumentally, even ignorantly: which of the competing candidates to vote for. In previous chapters we suggested that the uninformed choices of voters merely reflect the current disorganization of the electoral process and the accurate public perception that there are more appropriate opportunities for instrumental participation outside the electoral process than within it. This may help explain Sidney Verba and Norman Nie's findings that "data on the relative lack of instrumental orientation towards the vote contrasted sharply with . . . data on citizen-initiated contacts."[1]

Here we return to examine the hypothesis central to this study, namely, that it is the beneficiaries of the system who tend to vote, doing so as a symbolic gesture through which they confirm and reaffirm their commitment to the system. In other words, as elections have assumed a vestigial and peripheral role in affecting policy outcomes, they have come to be recognized for what they really are—political rituals—by those whose advantageous position in society makes them willing (perhaps even requires them) to engage in public gestures of political allegiance and conformity. Parallels with other ritualistic actions abound. For instance, while stalwart members of a community may attend church regularly on Sundays, their presence does not necessarily indicate a belief in God; it might simply reflect support of the advantageously situated for an institution that maintains a social order of which they approve.

We also intend to expand on the hypothesis that those without the political resources and skills to participate extra-electorally register their alienation from the system by *not* voting. Indeed, the "have-nots" have tended to abstain from voting even after specific prohibitions against their doing so have been lifted, despite intensive and often successful efforts to register them, and even after considerable exhortation to persuade them of voting's instrumental significance. Frustrated by the futility of the act, but without the resources or skills to engage in more complex contacting activities through extra-electoral channels, those on the lowest rungs of the socioeconomic ladder have tended to abandon the political arena entirely, except for intermittent and sporadic episodes that have been vividly described as "charged with paranoia and overt hostility."[2] Much of that activity is only proto-political, as was the case with the riots in Detroit, Newark, Watts, and other cities in the 1960s and more recently in Miami. More often, other random and violent acts such as rapes, muggings, and vandalism serve as substitutes for political action. Since in the United States the have-nots do not participate in the electoral process, their decision to abstain can be construed as a statement of disaffection from a political system from which they have been unable to extract material rewards.

The first part of our discussion describes the demographic profiles of voters and compares them with "contactors." The second part explores their motivations in going to the polls. Data for this investigation was obtained largely from three sources: (1) The Current Population Surveys conducted by the Census Bureau (the size and representativeness of the samples these surveys employ make them well suited to an investigation of this sort); (2) the National Election Studies conducted at the University of Michigan's Center for Political Studies (especially useful for obtaining insights into the motives of voters); and (3) a smaller postelection survey of 314 respondents in southern New Jersey, conducted by the author in March 1981.

Who Votes—The Variables

Several studies have indicated that voters tend to be atypical demographically of the population at large.[3] Those of middle and upper socioeconomic status and those of middle age tend to be overrepresented. Our task first is to present and update information on the demographic profiles of voters as a prelude to a more extended discussion of voter motivations.

Education. One of the strongest correlates of voter turnout is education.[4] As Figure 4A shows, the differential between those with the least education (0–4 years) and those with the most education (4+ years of college) is 50 percentage points. Although the gap narrowed somewhat in 1980 (see Figure 4B), the difference is still significant. Only in the United States has education been found to correlate significantly with voting (.21). Gabriel Almond and Sidney Verba's earlier five-nation cross-national study indicated either no correlation or a negative correlation in other countries, especially the less developed ones.[5] For example, in India the coefficient was −.04; in Japan it was .03 and in Nigeria −.03. In those countries, other studies have

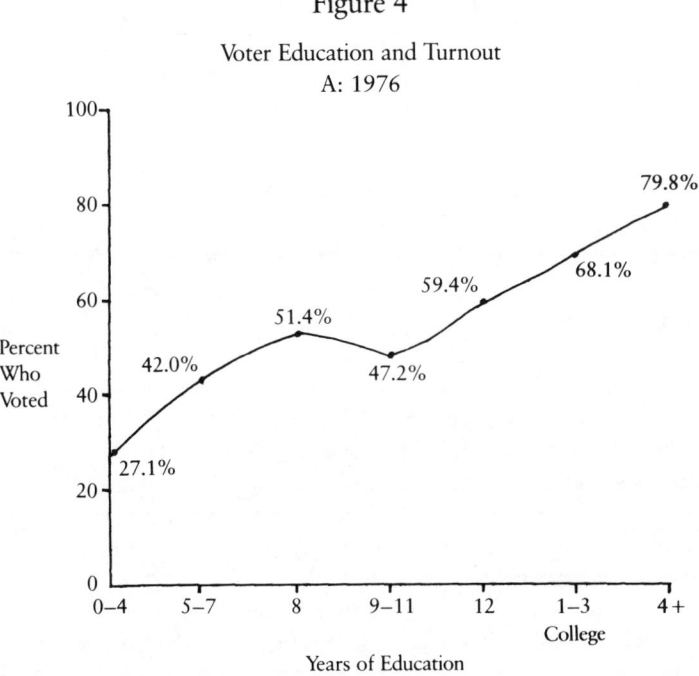

Figure 4

Voter Education and Turnout
A: 1976

Source: Charles E. Johnson, *Non-voting Americans* (Washington, D.C.: U.S. Department of Commerce, Bureau of the Census, 1977), p. 13.

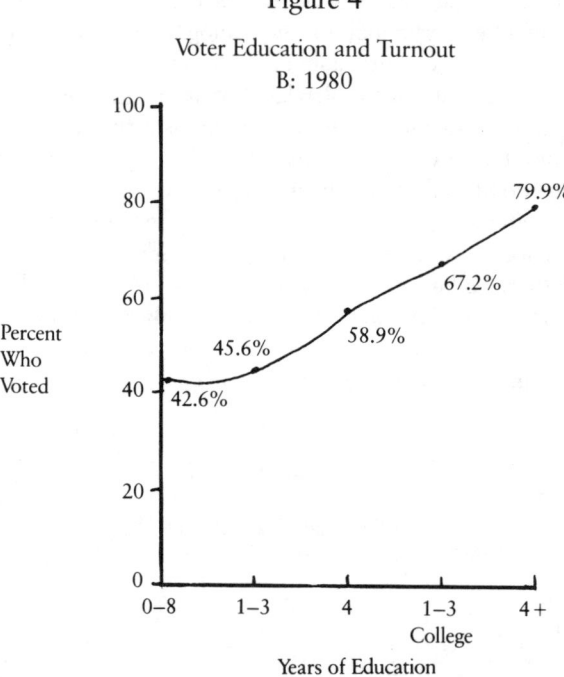

Figure 4

Voter Education and Turnout
B: 1980

Source: U.S. Bureau of the Census, Current Population Reports, Series P-20, No. 370, *Voting and Registration in the Election of November 1980* (Washington, D.C.: U.S. Government Printing Office, 1982).

suggested that the informed and knowledgeable are also more hostile to the system and less patriotic, and hence less likely to confirm their allegiance to the political system by voting. By way of contrast, the more permeable political system of the United States is, we assume, more likely to produce the feeling on the part of those who have the resources for effective participation that the government produces for them, reinforcing their feelings of allegiance to the system.[6]

Income. With respect to income, the differential voting rates between those at the top of the socioeconomic ladder and those at the bottom are not as dramatic, but they are still consistent with the observation that the beneficiaries of the system are the most likely to vote (see Figure 5). In 1976 there was a difference of slightly over 30 percent between the turnout rates of

Figure 5

Voter Income and Turnout
A: 1976

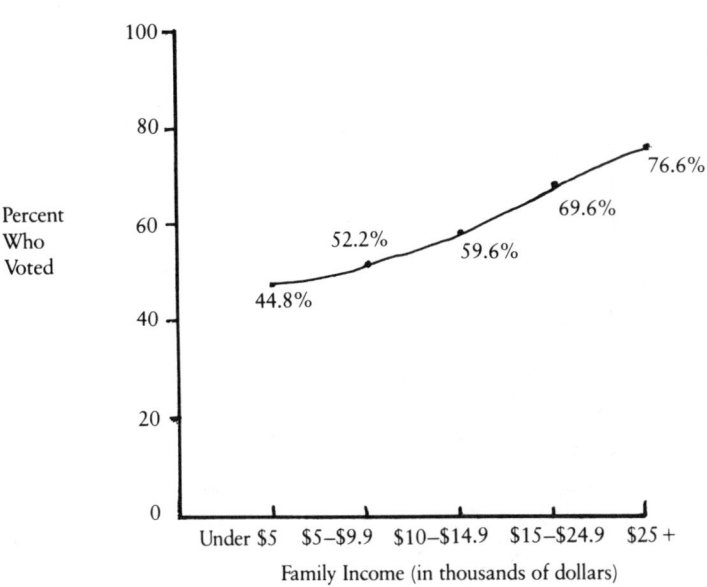

Source: Charles E. Johnson, *Non-Voting Americans* (Washington, D.C.: U.S. Department of Commerce, Bureau of the Census, 1977), p. 15.

those earning under $5,000 and those earning $25,000 and over (44.8% vs. 76.6% in 1976), while in 1980 the difference widened to 34.4% (39.4% vs. 73.8%).

Age. The finding that voting levels peak in middle age is shown in Figure 6. As the graph shows, people in the 55–64 age-group are likely to turn out about twice as frequently as those 18–20 years old, a group we shall call the "not-yet-haves" (38% vs. 69% in 1976). Little difference was found in the 1980 data.

Race. Although the aggregate reported turnout differentials between blacks and whites are not as large as one might expect (10–15%), when age is combined with race, black nonvoting rises dramatically. The rate of nonvoting among those who were poor and young, for instance, was 25.3 percent

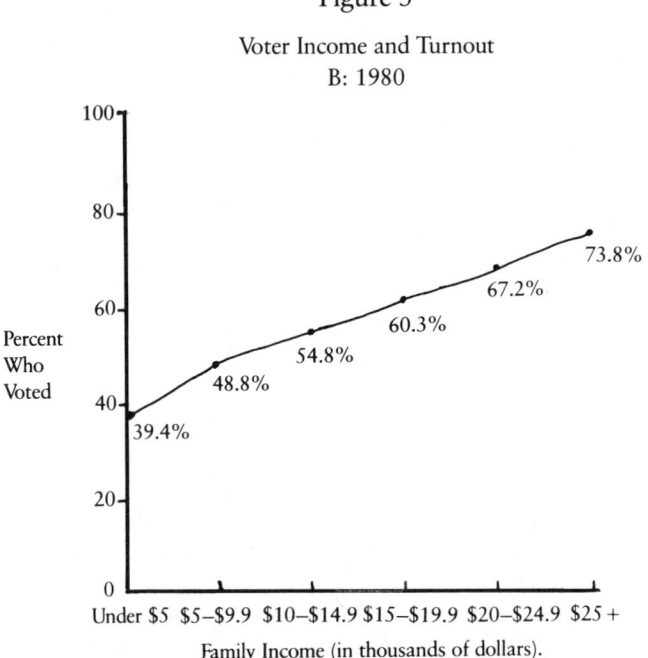

Figure 5

Voter Income and Turnout
B: 1980

Source: U.S. Bureau of the Census, Current Population Reports, Series P-20, No. 370, *Voting and Registration in the Election of November 1980* (Washington, D.C.: U.S. Government Printing Office, 1982).

in 1980 (see Figure 7). It should be noted, however, that even though blacks, on average, do vote 10 to 15 percent less than whites, those minorities who do vote are (like whites) more likely to be "connected" to the system. For instance, they are more likely to be older (61.5% of those between 45 and 65 years old voted in 1980, as opposed to 25.3% of those in the 18–20 age-group), more educated (81% of those with five or more years of college voted in 1980, compared with 41.2% of those with 0–4 years of schooling) (see Figure 8), and more likely to work for the government (68.3%) or for themselves (63.4%) than either privately employed wage earners (51.4%) or those in the agricultural sector (28.2%) (see Table 8). In other words, race is not as important as socioeconomic status, but minorities are disproportionately located at lower socioeconomic levels.

The Symbolism of Elections and the Ritualism of Voting

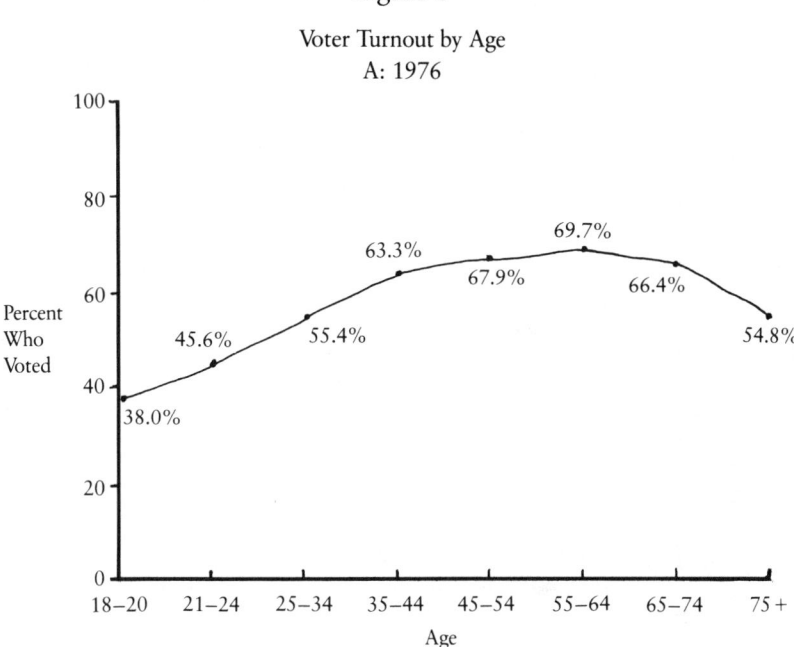

Figure 6

Voter Turnout by Age
A: 1976

Source: U.S. Bureau of the Census, Current Population Reports, Series P-20, No. 370, *Voting and Registration in the Election of November 1976* (Washington, D.C.: U.S. Government Printing Office, 1977).

Thus the demographic profile of the typical American voter (someone who is relatively well-off, well-educated, and middle-aged) is consistent with the profile of a person who is more likely than not to feel comfortable within, and hence to identify with, the status quo. More important, he or she is likely to have the skills and resources needed to operate competently within the complex political system by engaging either individually or with others in direct citizen-initiated contacts with decision-makers. At a minimum, he or she is likely to have a well-developed sense of personal efficacy. It is therefore not surprising that political incompetents will tend to be drawn disproportionately from the ranks of the poor, the young, and those who by virtue of their race have been denied educational opportunities and thus may

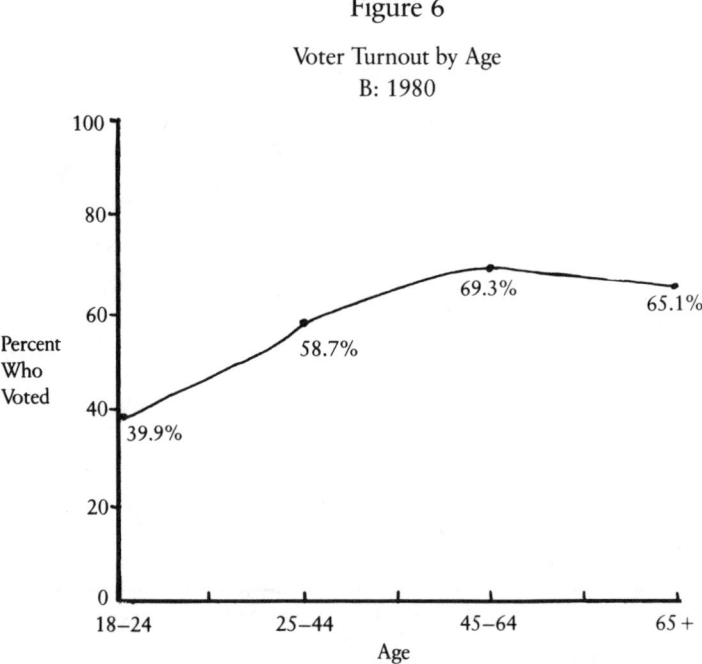

Figure 6

Voter Turnout by Age
B: 1980

Source: U.S. Bureau of the Census, Current Population Reports, Series P-20, No. 370, *Voting and Registration in the Election of November 1980* (Washington, D.C.: U.S. Government Printing Office, 1982).

not possess the political sophistication and technical expertise required for effective political action.

Empirical evidence has long confirmed the intuitive generalization that the class bias of objective political competence (demonstrated by participation in extra-electoral contacting forms of political activity) as well as subjective competence (a sense of political efficacy) mirrors the socioeconomic bias of voting. For example, in the author's New Jersey survey, of those responding affirmatively to a question asking "Have you ever contacted a public official about some issue or problem?" many more college-educated respondents (42.5%) claimed to have contacted a public official than those who did not graduate from high school (10%). Educational gaps between the

Figure 7

A: Voter Turnout by Race, 1976 and 1980

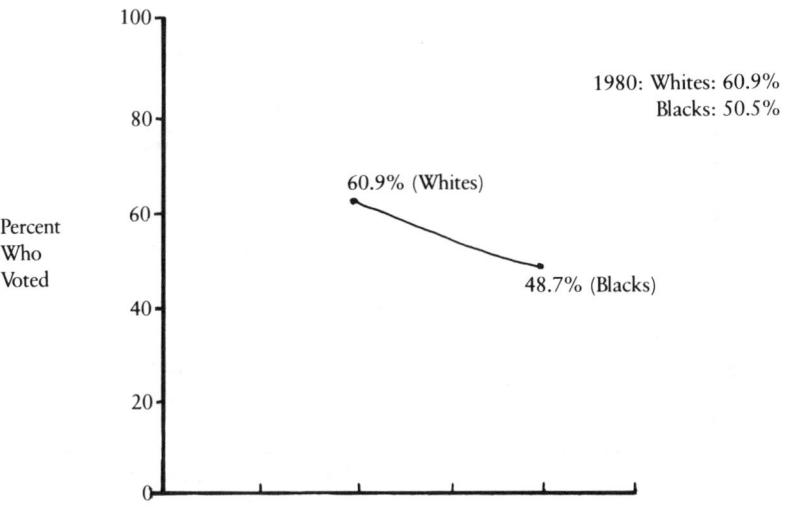

Source: U.S. Bureau of the Census, Current Population Reports, Series P-20, No. 370, *Voting and Registration in the Election of November 1976 and 1980* (Washington, D.C.: U.S. Government Printing Office, 1977 and 1982).

haves and have-nots apparently surface early. Studies of political socialization in children indicate that middle-class children possess more political knowledge than do lower-class children. This in turn affects their objective competence within the political system later on. As Robert Weissberg argues, "Even if participation levels were identical, the middle class's greater knowledge and sophistication might give it an advantage."[7] Our findings generally confirm those based on larger survey samples, such as Sidney Verba and Norman Nie's *Participation in America*, which found that 57 percent of the most politically active were from upper-status backgrounds and 14 percent were from lower-status backgrounds.[8] In the New Jersey data, 47.6 percent of those earning over $20,000 had engaged in "contacting," as opposed to only 12.8 percent of those earning under $10,000 (see Table 9).[9] Age, however, was the variable having the strongest effect on "contacting." According

Figure 7

B: Black Voter Turnout by Age, 1980

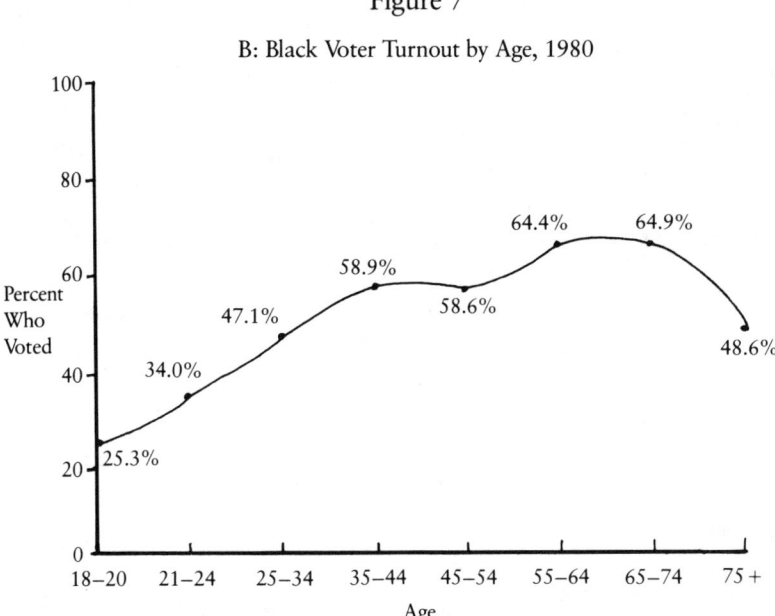

Source: U.S. Bureau of the Census, Current Population Reports, Series P-20, No. 370, *Voting and Registration in the Election of November 1980* (Washington, D.C.: U.S. Government Printing Office, 1982).

to the New Jersey data, 52 percent of those in the 35–64 age-group had been "contactors," compared with 18.9 percent of those in the 18–24 age-group.

With respect to race, Verba and Nie reported that "of the conditions under which individuals might contact the government [we] have found a greater likelihood that whites would contact the government despite the greater level of need among blacks."[10] Part of the reason for this is that blacks, as children, are socialized toward greater levels of apathy. For instance, an early study indicated that only 19.6 percent of black high school seniors were politically active, compared with 40 percent of whites.[11] More recently, Weissberg found that this "participation gap" increased with age, "so that as more and more white children come to perceive the political system as amenable to their influence, fewer and fewer blacks share this view."[12] Another part of the reason blacks are less likely to be politically

The Symbolism of Elections and the Ritualism of Voting

Figure 8

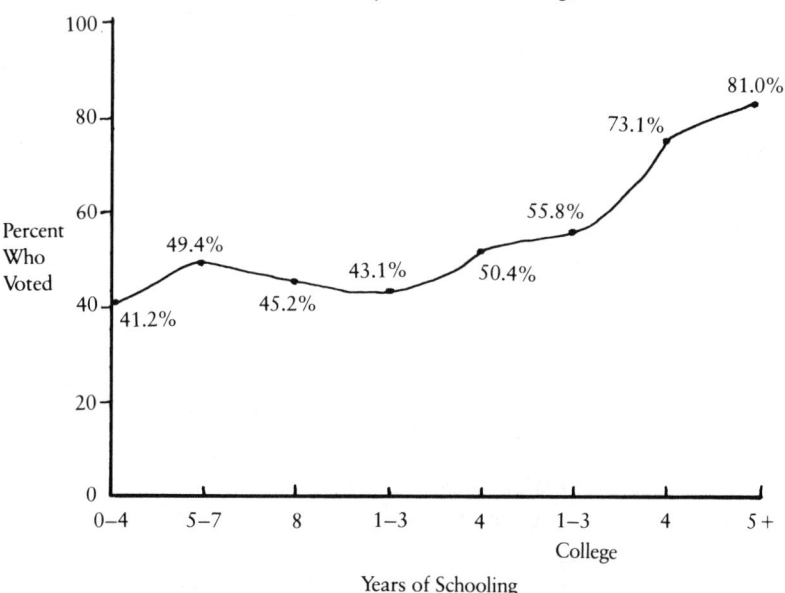

Black Voter Turnout by Years of Schooling, 1980

Source: U.S. Bureau of the Census, Current Population Reports, Series P-20, No. 370, *Voting and Registration in the Election of November 1980* (Washington, D.C.: U.S. Government Printing Office, 1982).

Table 8

Voting by Blacks According to Employment Status, 1980

Government workers	68.3%
Self-employed workers	63.4%
Privately employed wage and salaried workers	51.4%
Agricultural workers	28.2%
Unemployed	41.4%

Source: U.S. Bureau of the Census, Current Population Reports, Series P-20, No. 370, *Voting and Registration in the Election of 1980* (Washington, D.C.: U.S. Government Printing Office, 1982).

Table 9

Demographic Distribution of Contactors, 1981[a]

Upper Socioeconomic Status		Lower Socioeconomic status	
Some college/ college graduates	42.5%	8th grade or less	10.0%
35–64 years	52.0%	18–24 years	18.9%
Over $20,000	47.6%	Under $10,000	12.8%

Source: Data from author's New Jersey survey.
[a] $N = 103$

active is that blacks appear to have less political knowledge than whites. Thus, "even if blacks were as willing as whites to be active politically their lack of knowledge about government would prevent equally effective action through normal channels of political influence."[13]

Research also confirms that feelings of *subjective* political competence are linked with socioeconomic status; that is, feelings of political efficacy are found disproportionately among Americans whose *objective* socioeconomic positions are higher. Responses to a question on personal efficacy asked by the Survey Research Center at the University of Michigan demonstrate this.[14]

The statement "Sometimes politics and government are so complicated that a person like me can't really understand what's going on" was incorporated into a subjective efficacy scale by Almond and Verba. Their five-nation study showed that only 47 percent of those with "some primary level education" declared themselves subjectively competent, compared with 82 percent of those with "some university" education.[15]

One of the earliest studies, by Angus Campell et al., showed a strong relationship between sense of personal efficacy and the vote, a finding that remains valid today. On a political efficacy scale ranging from low to high, the authors found that 91 percent of those with a high sense of political efficacy also voted, while only 9 percent of those expressing such self-confidence did not vote. On the other hand, only about 52 percent of those expressing a low sense of political efficacy voted.[16]

In sum, voting, participation, and sense of political efficacy are all linked to socioeconomic status. Given the fact that it is "smart folks who vote dumb," while they perform other nonelectoral acts of participation instrumentally and competently, we have chosen to account for their decision to go to the polls at all as a rational choice to engage in what amounts to an act of legitimation. The evidence for this hypothesis follows.

Why People Vote

The possibility that voting was an expression of political allegiance was first suggested by rational-choice theorists, who viewed the decision to vote in terms of formal models assessing the relative costs and benefits to the individual voter. It was generally conceded by William Riker[17] and Gordon Tullock[18] that the instrumental benefits obtained from voting—chiefly the satisfaction of seeing a preferred candidate win—were outweighed by the costs incurred, given the small probability that a single individual's vote would influence the election outcome. In an attempt to account for the rationality of turnout, expressive benefits obtained from the decision to vote began to be included in voting equations. For example, Riker argued that one of the noninstrumental benefits accruing to the voter is the "halo effect"—the satisfaction that comes from affirming one's allegiance to, or efficacy in, the political system.[19] On the other hand, Tullock suggested that the main motive in going to the polls was a response to social pressure to perform one's duty as a citizen.[20]

Empirical evidence appears to confirm the logical deductions of rational-choice theory which concluded that voters were motivated to vote primarily for expressive reasons. And as we shall see, such motivations tend to increase with socioeconomic status.

In the first place, there is strong evidence of heavy symbolic commitment to elections and voting, despite awareness of alternative forms of political participation and despite a declining belief in the efficacy of elections. For example, even though 53 percent of respondents in 1976 disagreed with the statement "voting is the only way people like me can have a say about how the government runs things" (compared with only 30 percent a decade earlier) and despite indications that in 1976 some 14 percent fewer people than in 1964 thought that "elections help a good deal to make the government pay attention to what people think" (Tables 10 and 11), a consistently stable 88/89 percent disagreed with the statement "So many people vote in the national elections that it doesn't matter much to me whether I vote or not" over a thirty-year period (Table 12).

Table 10

Responses to Statement on Extra-electoral Participation, 1966 and 1976

"Voting is the only way that people like me can have a say about how the government runs things."

	1966[a]	1976[b]	Change
Strongly agree	58%	43%	(−15%)
Agree			
Disagree	30%	53%	(+23%)
Strongly disagree			
Neutral	10%	2%	
Don't know	2%	2%	

Sources: 1966 Wisconsin data from Jack Dennis, "Support for the Institution of Elections by the Mass Public, "*American Political Science Review* 64 (1970): 829. The 1976 data are from *American National Election Study Series*, 1976.
[a] $N = 607$
[b] $N = 3,004$

Table 11

Responses to Question on Efficacy of Elections, 1964 and 1976

Q: How much do you feel that elections help to make the government pay attention to what people think?

	1964[a]	1976[b]	Change
A good deal	65%	51%	−14%
Some	25%	35%	+10%
Not much	6%	10%	+ 4%
Don't know	4%	4%	0%

Source: Data from *American National Election Study Series*, 1964; 1976.
[a] $N = 1,450$
[b] $N = 2,403$

Table 12

Responses to Question on Concern About Voting

Q: "So many people vote in the national elections that it doesn't matter much to me whether I vote or not."

	1952	1956	1960	1976
Disagree[a]	86 %	89 %	89 %	88 %
Actual vote[b]	61.6%	59.3%	62.8%	54.4%

[a]*Source:* Data from *American National Election Study Series*, 1952; 1976.
[b]*Source:* Charles E. Johnson, *Non-voting Americans* (Washington, D.C.: U.S. Bureau of the Census, 1977), p. 13.

That participating in elections is a norm honored for its symbolic value rather than its practical value is indicated by Table 12, which shows that the actual rates of voting between 1952 and 1976 averaged 59.5 percent. More important, belief in the norm of electoral participation parallels the demographic biases of the voting population, particularly with respect to education. On a set of statements measuring commitment to the norm of electoral participation (see Figure 9) some 66 percent of those with five or more years of college expressed such commitment, as opposed to only 42 percent of those with 0–4 years of education.

The evidence thus far indicates only that upper-status individuals value voting more, and turn out in greater numbers, than lower-status individuals. We will now attempt to substantiate the hypothesis that these beneficiaries vote as an expression of their obligation and allegiance to the political system. Up to this point, studies have only hinted at the possibility, and with fragmentary empirical evidence. For instance, a study by Jack Dennis in 1970 concluded that "belief in elections as an effective instrument of participatory democracy [was] apparently lower in America than the belief that one should vote—something which would tend to increase the ritualistic aspects of electoral behavior."[21] This belief that voting is a kind of confirmation of good citizenship is also reflected in several of the interviews conducted by Robert E. Lane. He quotes one respondent as saying: "Oh gee, I think I'm a perfect citizen. Oh, sure, I mean, naturally, I try to—I vote as many times as I can."[22]

More recently, Lester Milbrath and M. L. Goel, in a revised version of

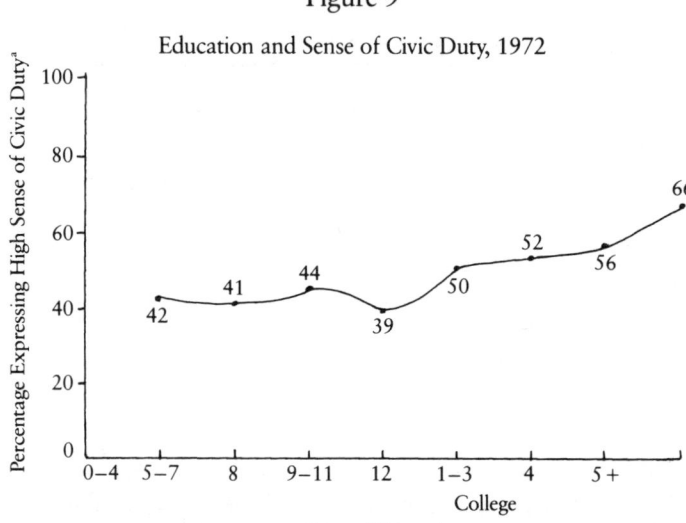

Figure 9

Education and Sense of Civic Duty, 1972

Source: Adapted from Steven J. Rosenstone and Raymond E. Wolfinger, *Who Votes?* (New Haven: Yale University Press, 1980), p. 19. By permission of Yale University Press.

[a]Respondents who disagreed with these statements: "It isn't so important to vote when you know your party doesn't have a chance to win." "So many people vote that it doesn't matter much to me whether I vote or not." "If a person doesn't care how an election comes out, he shouldn't vote in it." "A good many local elections aren't important enough to bother with."

an earlier and well-received study retitled *Political Participation* (1977), presented the findings of a 1968 survey of voters in Buffalo, New York:

Voting clustered with other patriotic acts: "love my country"; "show my patriotism by flying the flag"; "pay all taxes"; "respect the police"; "support my country in wars I don't agree with." This clustering indicates that voting is more an act by which a citizen affirms his loyalty to the system rather than an act by which he makes demands on the system.[23]

Milbrath and Goel also found that people who voted rarely believed that their vote would make a difference but voted anyway out of a sense of civic duty.

The data from the author's New Jersey survey does provide more direct insights into voter motivations and confirms Milbrath and Goel's findings concerning the importance of "civic duty" as a motivating factor (see Table 13). When respondents were asked an open-ended question, "Why did you vote in the last election?" the obligation to vote—"civic duty"—outweighed any other instrumental reasons for voting, such as candidate preference (14%), perceived "need for a change" (9%), or party preference (2%) by a wide margin (56%). It even outweighed one of the more conventional noninstrumental reasons academics assume impels voting—"habit." Only 15 percent of the New Jersey sample named "habit" as a reason for voting. It is important to emphasize the distinction between "habit" and "civic duty." The former is a repetitive act performed without much conscious motivation, while the latter indicates performance of an obligation rationally undertaken.

Demographic breakdowns of the subsample of respondents who chose "civic duty" as their primary reason for going to the polls confirm that the call of duty is more likely to be heeded by the beneficiaries of the system (the haves) than by the have-nots (see Table 14). While 41.5 percent of college-educated voters claimed "civic duty," only 17 percent of those with education of high school or less did so. In terms of income, 44 percent of those earning over $20,000 claimed "civic duty," while only 20 percent of those earning under $10,000 did so. Only in terms of age was our hypothesis apparently disconfirmed. Of those in the 18–24 age-group, 43 percent chose "civic duty," in contrast with 36 percent of those in the 35–64 age-group.

It should be noted, however, that Jack Dennis had reported similar results in his 1966 survey of Wisconsin residents, leading him to conclude that "the youngest adults feel their obligation to participate more strongly and

Table 13

Responses to the Question "Why Did You Decide to Vote?" 1981[a]

Civic duty	56%
Habit	15%
Candidate preference	14%
Need for a change	9%
Party preference	2%
No response	5%

Source: Data from author's New Jersey survey.
[a] $N = 238$. Does not add up to 100% due to errors of rounding.

Table 14

Demographic Distribution of Responses Claiming "Civic Duty" as Reason for Voting, 1981

Education	
College/some college	41.5%
High school or less	17.0%
Age	
35–64	36.3%
25–34	15.6%
18–24	43.0%
Income	
Over $20,000	44%
Under $10,000	20%

Source: Data from author's New Jersey survey.
[a] N = 135

more fully approve of the electoral process."[24] Our own tentative explanation for this finding is that it probably reflects the lingering effects of high school socialization in which civics courses strongly emphasize the norm of voting.

The University of Michigan Survey Research Center data, underscoring the passive and expressive orientation toward voting, indicate that while citizens are prepared to go to the polls, they are willing to do little else (see Table 15). In 1976 an extremely small minority (under 10 percent) of respondents reported any other form of electoral participation, such as giving money, helping candidates, or going to meetings or rallies. This minimal operational support for elections is further reflected in the Survey Research Center's question concerning political discussion (see Table 16). Whereas *after* the presidential election of 1976, some 80 percent of respondents claimed to have talked about the results to someone else, when asked (in the same postelection survey) whether they had talked about the campaign *during* the election, only 36 percent reported having done so. One reason for the dramatic difference in reported public interest may lie in the wording of the two questions. The former question asked respondents only whether they

Table 15

Responses to Questions on Operational Support, 1976[a]

	Yes	No	NA
During the campaign did you go to any political meetings, rallies, dinners, or things like that?	6%	93%	3%
During the campaign did you do any other work for one of the parties or candidates?	7%	92%	1%
Did you give any money to a political party or make any other contribution this year?	8% + 7% (tax checkoff)[b]	83%	1%

Source: Data from *American National Election Study Series*, 1976.
[a] $N = 2,403$. Some rows do not add up to 100% due to errors of rounding.
[b] Contributions made on income tax returns to the Presidential Election Fund.

had discussed the election results, while the question posed about discussion during the campaign also asked whether respondents had "tried to show [others] why they should vote for one of the parties and candidates." Political persuasion, as opposed to discussion, involves an active orientation and was engaged in by far fewer respondents.

From the perspective that elections are rituals and voting is a symbolic act performed by the system's beneficiaries, not an instrumental act, several puzzling aspects of political participation become more understandable. For example, Richard Brody's study showed that voters who found the choice of candidates totally unappealing were only slightly less likely to vote than those who found the choices pleasing (see Table 17).[25] Some 78.6 percent of "concerned" citizens voted, compared with 70 percent of "aliented" citizens, a difference of only 8.6 percent. From the perspective that voting has little to do with making informed choices and more to do with legitimation,

Table 16

Passive vs. Active Interest in Elections, 1976

	Yes	No	NA
After the presidential election, did you talk with anyone about how the election came out?	80%	19%	1%
During the campaign, did you talk to any people and try to show them why they should vote for one of the parties and candidates?	36%	63%	1%

Source: Data from *American National Election Study Series,* 1976. Michigan.
[a]N = 2,403

Table 17

Expected and Observed Rates of Turnout for Different Candidate Evaluation Groups, 1972

	Candidate Evaluation Groups/Feelings About Candidates				
	Concerned	Satisfied	Satisfied/ Indifferent	Alienated	Alienated/ Indifferent
Expected to vote	84.3%	76.0%	76.7%	79.2%	77.8%
Actually voted	78.6%	69.2%	73.0%	70.0%	68.8%
Difference	5.7%	6.8%	3.7%	9.2%	9.0%

Source: Adapted from Richard A. Brody, "The Puzzle of Participation," in *The New American Political System,* ed. Anthony King (Washington, D.C.: American Enterprise Institute, 1978), p. 311. Used by permission of the American Enterprise Institute.
Data derived from applying the Brody-Sniderman model to data from *American National Election Study Series,* 1972.

Brody's analysis seems to confirm that those who decide to vote do so regardless of the choices offered them.

Moreover, as the study by Angus Campbell and his associates indicates, the level of interest in the election itself has little to do with turnout. Although those who are most interested turn out more, 59 percent of those who were "not much interested" also voted, as did 52 percent who "didn't care at all."[26] By the same token, the cynical (but not the alienated) are as likely to turn out as the trusting. Using "trust in government" as an indicator of cynicism (which represents lack of support for the incumbent administration rather than a lack of regime support),[27] Richard Brody and Paul Sniderman found that "it has proved exceedingly difficult to find any such relationship among the citizenry at large. When we examine the [turnout] data, we observe scarcely any difference between the politically cynical and the politically trusting."[28] That neither lack of interest in the election nor cynicism with respect to elected officials has any bearing on the decision to vote seems to underscore our findings that voting is performed first and foremost as a civic duty.

The lower socioeconomic status of nonvoters and their abstention from other extra-electoral participatory acts suggests that they are less likely to conform to, or to perform, their civic obligations. Some have-nots of course do vote. Perhaps that is because not all have-nots will objectively define themselves as being deprived, while others may be "aspiring haves," who identify with the system and hope some day to be able to extract material rewards from it. Socioeconomic background does not totally predict political behavior. Personality variables (and personal idiosyncrasies) must also be taken into account if we are to explain why some have-nots who might be expected to abstain do vote.

But many of those on the lowest rungs of the socioeconomic ladder will feel alienated from the political system. Why? It has been suggested that many have-nots have been inadequately influenced by socialization agencies that both affect political consciousness and inculcate positive feelings toward the political system early in life. Family structure for such a group is often weak, have-nots often drop out of school early, ties to the workplace are frequently nonexistent, and peer pressure to engage in anomic criminal activities is intense. As David Schwartz has suggested, those not organizationally connected to the society are likely to get fewer rewards and, "if politics is a matter of who gets what, when, and how, people who get little from the system will value it less (i.e., be less allegiant) and be more alienated."[29] A recent study by Jack Citrin and Associates formulated a "political alienation index" that was cross-tabulated with socioeconomic data.[30] Their findings on various factors, listed below, clearly indicate that (on a scale of 1 through 5, where 1 is most allegiant and 5 most alienated) the people most likely to be alienated are those who have consistently received the fewest benefits from the system; allegiance is concentrated within the ranks of those at the upper end of the socioeconomic scale.

Income. The percentage of those in the highest income bracket who were most allegiant was almost double the percentage of those in the lowest income bracket (27.5% in the $20,000+ groups, compared with 14% in those earning under $5,000).

Race. Whites were likely to be four times more allegiant than blacks (21.5% whites, 5.8% blacks), while at the alienated end of the scale, blacks were three times more alienated than whites (44.3% blacks, 14.4% whites).

Age. Approximately 25% of those age 50–60 scored at the most allegiant end of the scale, compared with only 8.5% of those between the ages of 18 and 25. Conversely, approximately 33% of those age 18–25 were placed at the most-alienated end of the scale, compared with only 12% of those in the 50–60 age-group.

Occupation. In keeping with the rest of the findings, 30.3% of the managerial group were placed on the most-allegiant end of the scale, compared with a scant 10.6% of the unskilled labor group. In fact, the latter obtained the highest percentage score on the alienated end of the scale (25.5%).

The Citrin study is the most recent in a long line of studies investigating the socioeconomic dimensions of allegiance and alienation, and it confirms the earlier and more dramatic findings that emerged from the reports of presidential commissions that followed the campus riots and ghetto violence during the 1960s. For example, the National Advisory Commission on Civil Disorders (the Kerner Commission) discovered particularly high levels of alienation among blacks who had participated in the rioting. One measure of this alienation was the response to the question asking ghetto respondents whether they thought "this country was worth fighting for in the event of a major world war." Some 39.4 percent of self-reported rioters in Detroit and 52.8 percent in Newark reported that it was not.[31]

The young (the not-yet-haves) also tend to be less allegiant, although what was perhaps the peak of such sentiment was tapped by a 1968 Harris poll in which 75 percent of students expressed a belief that "basic changes in the system would be necessary to improve the quality of life in the United States."[32] While such sentiments may be expressed by fewer young people today, the Citrin study indicates that there is still a latent reservoir of such attitudes among the not-yet-haves.

Since the very poor, the young, and the minorities tend to be excluded from the processes by which tangible benefits are actually distributed, it is unlikely that they would turn out to vote. Indeed, participation in protest activity is highest among those lowest in more conventional forms of participation. Analyzing survey data from the University of Michigan's Survey Research Center for 1976, Alan Abramowitz found that more young people reported protesting (18 percent) than working for a presidential candidate (13 percent). Moreover, more blacks reported protesting (20 percent) than working for a presidential candidate (7 percent), writing to their congressperson (12 percent), or giving money to a political candidate (15 percent).[33]

We may use this as the key to solving the paradox noted by Steven Rosenstone and Raymond Wolfinger, who discovered that turnout levels have fallen at the same time that the electorate has expanded: "The modern peak of voter turnout was reached in 1960 when one- and two-year residency requirements, poll taxes and literacy tests were common; and when millions of southern blacks were disenfranchised through maladministration of the laws. Since then all these barriers have been removed . . . and turnout has fallen."[34] (See also Figure 10.) While the authors are unable to explain why turnout levels have fallen, it should be noted that the removal of barriers to voting, such as elimination of literacy requirements and poll taxes, brought into the electoral process groups who were also effectively prevented (by reason of incompetence and inexperience) from other more meaningful forms of participation. Moreover, the addition of the youth vote after 1972 (when eighteen-year-olds were enfranchised) has not helped raise voting levels. The young tend not to vote, possibly because they have little experience and a minimal stake in the system. As a result, voting levels have fallen despite an expansion of the electorate.

Other studies confirm our intuitive judgment that these have-nots and not-yet-haves will be unlikely to vote even if extensive efforts are made to register them. Charles Hamilton found that despite a massive and successful registration effort in Harlem by many nonpartisan civic groups, such as the Urban League and the NAACP, voter turnout on election day remained either stagnant or declined from previous levels. Moreover, new registrants from the black lower class turned out less (46 percent) than new registrants who were middle class (64.2 percent).[35]

There are some who claim that complex registration requirements constitute the main barrier to voting, particularly for the have-nots. One of the most vocal advocates for the remedy of universal voter registration, Penn Kimball, maintains:

Beyond the Electoral Connection

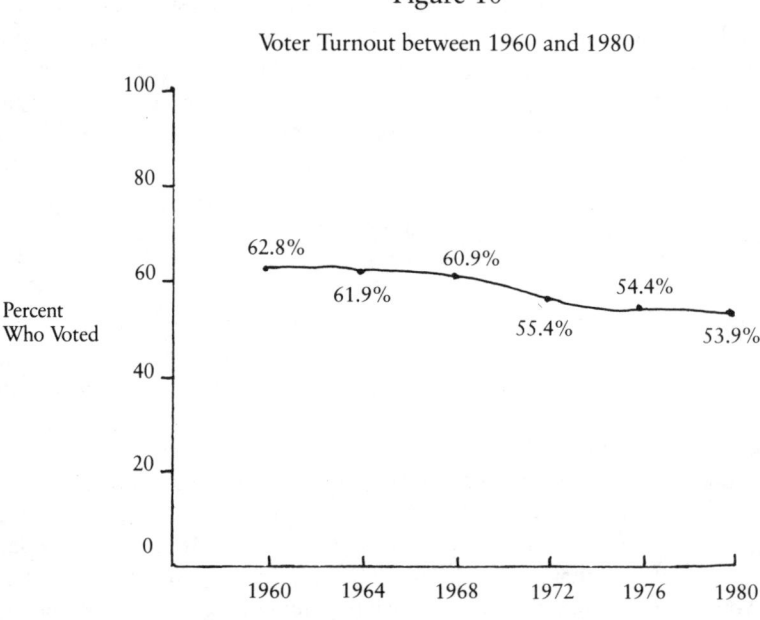

Figure 10

Voter Turnout between 1960 and 1980

Presidential Election Years

Source: U.S. Bureau of the Census, Current Population Reports, Series P-20, No. 370, *Voting and Registration in the Elections of November 1976 and 1980* (Washington, D.C.: Government Printing Office, 1977 and 1982).

The failure of the American political system to engage millions of potential voters is the product of the institutional structure by which persons can qualify to vote. And there will probably be no significant improvement in public participation in the electoral process until the Federal government takes the initiative to qualify eligible voters rather than place the onus upon individuals thwarted by outmoded state and local regulations. Voting in America is enmeshed in a spider's web of prior restraints.[36]

An earlier study had even estimated that as many as 10 million people would have liked to have voted but forgot to register.[37]

However, more recent evidence suggests that even without the existence of onerous registration requirements the have-nots will choose not to vote. Reform has not led to higher levels of turnout. For instance, by 1976 some seventeen states had made it easier to register by adopting registration by mail. Yet one study showed that voter turnout in those states actually *declined*.[38] In 1978 and 1981, Rosenstone and Wolfinger attempted to measure the political consequences of registration law reform by comparing the characteristics of the actual electorate to a hypothetical expanded electorate. They found that if every state had permissive registration laws, turnout would have been increased by only 9 percent. Comparing actual voters to hypothetical voters by projecting rates of change in turnout, they concluded, "Relaxing registration requirements would produce a voting population very similar to the actual 1972 voters. The number of voters would increase, but there would be virtually no change in their *demographic, partisan* or *ideological characteristics*. They would be more numerous, but not different."[39] In other words, the haves would continue to vote in greater numbers than the have-nots.

Since Rosenstone and Wolfinger are unable to explain why turnout levels would remain static even if voting is made easier, we again offer the alternative explanation, confirmed by our New Jersey data on "civic duty," that those who do not vote have probably made that choice because they recognize voting to be a symbolic act of reaffirmation, not one that will bring tangible benefits. Unable to obtain material rewards for themselves through more complex, nonelectoral channels, and hence alienated from the system, the have-nots feel little obligation to engage in acts of political ritualism to the extent that their middle-class counterparts do.

To suggest that elections in the United States are largely ritualistic exercises recognized as such by American citizens (and that voting is practiced as an act of middle-class conformity and allegiance) is to raise still further questions about the character, if not the viability, of American democracy. We now turn to an examination of that issue.

Notes

1. See Sidney Verba and Norman Nie, *Participation in America: Democracy and Social Equality* (New York: Harper & Row, 1972), p. 104.
2. See Guiseppi Di Palma, "Disaffection and Participation in Western Democracies: The Role of Oppositions," *Journal of Politics* 31 (November 1969): 984–1010.
3. The most recent and most well-documented such study is Steven J. Rosenstone and Raymond E. Wolfinger, *Who Votes?* (New Haven: Yale University Press, 1980). See also Seymour Martin Lipset, *Political Man: The Social Bases of Politics* (Garden City, N.Y.: Doubleday & Co., 1963), p. 189.

4. See Rosenstone and Wolfinger, *Who Votes?*, p. 17, as well as Angus Campbell et al., *The American Voter* (New York: John Wiley & Sons, 1960), pp. 476–78; Lester Milbrath, *Political Participation* (Chicago: Rand McNally & Co., 1965), pp. 122–23; and James Barber, *Citizen Politics: An Introduction to Political Behavior* (Chicago: Markham Publishing Co., 1969), pp. 11–14.
5. Gabriel Almond and Sidney Verba, *The Civic Culture* (Princeton: Princeton University Press, 1963), p. 167.
6. Lester Milbrath et al., *Political Participation* (Chicago: Rand McNally and Co., 1977), p. 100.
7. Robert Weissberg, *Political Learning, Political Choice, and Democratic Citizenship* (Englewood Cliffs, N.J.: Prentice-Hall, 1974), p. 101.
8. See Verba and Nie, *Participation in America*, p. 131. See also Robert Dahl, *Democracy in America: Promise and Performance* (Chicago: Rand McNally & Co., 1976), p. 450.
9. Compare the results of the 1965 Roper survey posing the question "Have you written to your congressman during the last 12 months?": Income $0–$4,999, 4.8%; $5,000–$9,999, 9.1%; $10,000–$14,999, 19.5%; over $15,000, 21% (% affirmative responses). Reported in David Mayhew, *Congress: The Electoral Connection* (New Haven: Yale University Press, 1974), p. 109.
10. See Almond and Verba, *The Civic Culture*, pp. 501–3.
11. Kent Jennings' study in Weissberg, *Political Learning*, p. 109.
12. Ibid.
13. Ibid., p. 111.
14. See the *American National Election Study 1976* (machine-readable data file), conducted by the Center for Political Studies, the University of Michigan, under the direction of Warren E. Miller and Arthur H. Miller. ICPSR ed. Ann Arbor, Mich.: Interuniversity Consortium for Political and Social Research, 1977.
15. Almond and Verba, *The Civic Culture*, p. 237.
16. Campbell et al., *The American Voter*, p. 105.
17. William Riker, "A Theory of the Calculus of Voting," *American Political Science Review* 62 (March 1968): 25–42.
18. Gordon G. Tullock, *Towards a Mathematics of Politics* (Ann Arbor: University of Michigan Press, 1968), chap. 2.
19. Riker, "A Theory of the Calculus of Voting," pp. 36–38.
20. Tullock, *Towards a Mathematics of Politics*, p. 114.
21. Jack Dennis, "Support for the Institution of Elections Among the Mass Public," *American Political Science Review* 64 (September 1970): 830.
22. Robert E. Lane, *Political Man* (New York: The Free Press, 1972), p. 285.
23. Milbrath and Goel, *Political Participation*, p. 12.
24. Dennis, "Support for the Institution of Elections," p. 830.

25. Richard A. Brody, "The Puzzle of Participation," in *The New American Political System*, ed. Anthony King (Washington, D.C.: American Enterprise Institute, 1978), p. 311.
26. Campbell et al., *The American Voter*, pp. 103–6.
27. As both Lester Milbrath and Edward Muller have cautioned, the two concepts of regime support and support for the incumbent administration are conceptually distinct. Political alienation is more deep-seated than cynicism because it questions the basic principles and norms of the polity. Thus rising levels of distrust for the incumbent administration do not necessarily reflect a denial of legitimacy or declining allegiance for the political system. See Milbrath et al., *Political Participation*, p. 64. See also Edward Muller and Thomas Jackson, "On the Meaning of Political Support," *American Political Science Review* 71 (December 1977): 1561–95.
28. See Richard Brody and Paul Sniderman, "From Life Space to Polling Place," *British Journal of Political Science* 7 (1977): 337–60.
29. David C. Schwartz, *Political Alienation and Political Behavior* (Chicago: Aldine Publishing Co., 1973), p. 9.
30. See Jack Citrin et al., "Personal and Political Sources of Political Alienation," *British Journal of Political Science* 5 (1975): 17.
31. *Report of the National Advisory Commission on Civil Disorders* (New York: Bantam Books, 1968), p. 135.
32. *Report of the President's Commission on Campus Unrest* (New York: Arno Press, 1970), p. 48.
33. Alan I. Abramowitz, "The United States: Political Culture Under Stress," in *The Civic Culture Revisited*, ed. Gabriel Almond and Sidney Verba (Boston: Little, Brown & Co., 1980), p. 200.
34. Steven J. Rosenstone and Raymond Wolfinger, "The Effect of Registration Laws on Voter Turnout," *American Political Science Review* 72 (March 1978): 41. See also idem, *Who Votes?*, chap. 4.
35. See Charles V. Hamilton, "Voter Registration Drives and Turnout: A Report on the Harlem Electorate," *Political Science Quarterly* 92 (Spring 1977): 46.
36. Penn Kimball, *The Disconnected* (New York: Columbia University Press, 1972), p. 3.
37. See Stanley Kelley, Jr., Richard E. Ayres, and William G. Bowen, "Registration and Voting: Putting First Things First," *American Political Science Review* 61 (June 1967): 359–79.
38. See Richard Smolka, *Election Day Registration: The Minnesota and Wisconsin Experience in 1976* (Washington, D.C.: American Enterprise Institute, 1977), p. 5.
39. Rosenstone and Wolfinger, *Who votes?*, p. 88. Emphasis added.

FIVE

THE ROLE OF ELECTIONS IN AMERICAN DEMOCRACY

The argument that elections in America have become essentially symbolic rituals, during which those who have benefited from the system in more direct ways vote to express their political support for the status quo, leads to the question "Can such a political system be called democratic?" Conventional usage, which tends to define political democracy in strictly electoral terms, suggests that the United States therefore ought not to be considered a democracy. Political scientists have long considered it "normal" to single out the institution of elections and to assume that it is primarily through voting that the average citizen influences policy and controls decision-makers. Thus, although other models of democracy exist, "contemporary discussions of the concept of democracy have employed elections as a primary definition and requisite feature of a democracy. Indeed, if any single institution serves as democracy's sine qua non it is that of elections."[1]

The problem is that despite the ubiquitous acceptance of this standard definition of democracy as necessarily representative in form, there is a widening gap in the United States between democratic theory (in which elections are supposed to play a major policy role) and empirical reality (in which elections are of symbolic significance only). With the decline of political parties, it is becoming embarrassingly obvious that the electoral process is effectively divorced from the political process, leaving the act of voting with only vestigial instrumental significance.

However, while many academics are still prepared to claim that elections in the United States do conform to their prescribed role, and although the public still pays lip service to their supposed instrumental importance, other informed observers (both consensus and revisionist) have begun to realize that the United States no longer conforms to the simple precepts of a representative democracy. Such grave doubts about the state of the electoral process have led to increasing concern about the viability of American democracy.

In the course of this study so far, we have expressed similar concerns about elections yet have retained the belief that America remains democratic. We intend now to resolve this apparent conceptual dilemma by seeking an alternative definition of the term "democracy."

Given that popular participation occurs continuously and outside electoral channels, we intend to suggest that American democracy can more appropriately be characterized as "citizen-participant" rather than representative in nature. Our departure from conventional usage, however, demands explanation, so we will begin by briefly investigating the origins and the intellectual liabilities of conventional conceptualizations of democracy as necessarily electoral, given the alternative modes by means of which citizen influence and control can be exercised. We shall also consider whether the primacy of the elected branches can be reasserted given the cultural, institutional, and organizational realities of contemporary American politics. Finally, the role elections do play in a nonelectoral democracy will be assessed.

The Origins of Representative Democracy

Although it has become common to define political democracy procedurally[2] (i.e., as a way of making decisions without regard for their content) as well as almost exclusively in electoral terms, it is important to recognize that this focus on "elections" is a relatively recent phenomenon. Until late in the nineteenth century the procedural emphasis in political conceptions of democracy did not necessarily preclude continuous mass involvement. Only later did a theoretical argument emerge that it was desirable to limit public participation to voting in elections. That particular conceptual narrowing has been attributed by Peter Bachrach to Joseph Schumpeter.[3] In his writings, Schumpeter strongly advised that popular participation should be minimal, so much so that some observers claim he twisted the normative ideal of "government by the people" into government "approved by the people." From this standpoint, elections assumed a primary role as the first and foremost step in the democratic process, and the most important act of citizenship became the one practiced in the voting booth. Having voted, the people were encouraged to leave all political decisions to their elected officials. As noted previously, Schumpeter carefully explained, "Voters . . . must respect the division of labor between themselves and the politicians they elect. . . . They must understand that once they have elected an individual, political action is his business, not theirs."[4] Theoretically, then, popular control over public policy became indirect. The people were now to confine their involvement in politics to choosing between competing elites, the representatives thus chosen to be held periodically and retroactively accountable for their actions. Voting became the principal participatory activity through which popular influence and control were to be exercised. Between elections the public was expected to remain politically inactive.

What Bachrach ignored was that Schumpeter had been both enormously influenced and overly impressed by the British model of representative democracy, which was based on a uniquely British conception of government as ideally coherent, organized, disciplined, and internally exempt from popular influence and control. As A. D. Lindsay, British political theorist, bluntly stated, "The organs of power in a democratic state are not and cannot well be themselves democratically organized."[5] He continued, implicitly explaining the reasons for a minimal public role confined to elections: "Government strictly understood is necessarily confined to the few. In that case the people cannot govern, but they can control."[6] As the primary means of exercising popular influence and control, elections were well suited to countries (like Great Britain) with institutional arrangements that were parliamentary in form and to political cultures that were, like Great Britain's, essentially elitist.

The transatlantic origins of modern normative conceptions of democracy have become deeply buried as British and American political scientists alike have embraced the "representative" model of democracy as standard. Hence elections and voting are now generally regarded as critical elements in defining a political democracy. This indirect or representative feature appears as a central point in C. B. McPherson's *The Real World of Democracy*: "How to make a government responsive to the choices of those it was expected to cater to? *The* way was of course to put governmental power into the hands of men *who were made subject to periodic elections at which there was a choice of candidates and parties.*"[7] It reappears in Dorothy Pickles' definition of democracy as a system of government that fills two essential requirements:

The Role of Elections in American Democracy

It must first be able to elicit as accurately as possible the opinions of as many people as possible on *who should be their representatives*. . . . This means, at a minimum, universal suffrage, political parties and the organization of free voting in uncorrupt elections at frequent intervals. Second, it must provide ways of ensuring that those chosen by the people do in fact do what the electorate wants them to do or that they can be replaced even between elections.[8]

Similarly, J. Roland Pennock defines democracy in exclusively electoral terms:

A democracy is rule by the people. . . . "Rule" means that public policies are determined either by vote of the electorate or indirectly by officials freely elected at reasonably frequent intervals and by a process in which each voter who chooses to vote counts equally ("one person, one vote") and in which a plurality is determinative.[9]

It even appears as a central argument in the work of American political theorist Robert M. MacIver, who echoed the British model when he wrote:

Representative democracy, the only kind that has any meaning under modern conditions, does not put any impossible strain on the citizen. . . . The people, let us repeat, do not and cannot, govern; they control the government. In every live democracy they decide the broad march of politics [and] . . . they decide issues, not one at a time, but by voting for an administration favorable to one or another platform.[10]

Two more contemporary figures, Robert Dahl and Anthony Downs, have spelled out similar notions of what political democracy is by also emphasizing elections and voting. Enumerating some requirements for a democracy, Dahl included "the right to vote," eligibility for "public office," "the right of political leaders to compete for votes," and "free and fair elections" as definitive indicators.[11] And Anthony Downs had earlier recognized similar electoral conditions for a democratic political system.[12]

The pervasive influence of the British model can also be observed in empirical democratic theory. For example, the classic study by Seymour Martin Lipset, *Political Man* (an empirical examination of the social and economic factors that make democracy possible), defined the concept of democracy in strictly Schumpeterian terms as "a social mechanism which permits the largest possible part of the population to influence the major decisions by choosing among contenders for political office."[13] Having conceptualized it in this manner, the empirical indicators used by Lipset were exclusively electoral—for example, percentage of the population voting and competitiveness of party systems.

Subsequent attempts to estimate empirically the extent of "political democracy" have followed Lipset's example by operationalizing it exclusively in electoral terms. For example, Deane Neubauer, utilizing a sample of twenty-three democratic nations to test the effect of socioeconomic development on democratic government, devised an index of democratic development which "concentrates mainly on electoral features of democratic regimes."[14]

It is not that other forms of political participation do not exist. It is merely that for theoretical purposes they are considered secondary in estimating the presence or absence of political democracy. As Dennis Thompson explains, "Forms of participation which permit a more direct role in decision-making and those which take place outside regular channels [exist]. But these less common forms of participation are *beyond the will and beyond the reach of most citizens most of the time* in modern democracies."[15]

Is the United States a Representative Democracy?

It is remarkable that most American political scientists, consensus and revisionists alike, have assumed that theoretical conceptions of democracy, derived from the British model, could be imposed on American practice. They have almost totally ignored the political arrangements and cultural preconceptions unique to the United States which prevent elections from playing their normatively defined role as critical linkage events. As a result, American political science generally has been unable to explain why the evidence of contemporary participatory behavior contradicts the assumptions of traditional democratic theory.

Still those assumptions—that elections are a defining characteristic of a democracy and that voting in them is instrumentally important—are widely and unquestioningly accepted. Gerald Pomper cavalierly dismisses any reassessment to the contrary by declaring that the relationship between elections and democracy is "obvious, even tautological,"[16] while ten years earlier he had insisted that "elections are a unique institution of democracy and a viable democracy requires meaningful elections."[17] Pomper is by no means alone in accepting the assumptions of the British model of democracy. James D. Barber in an introductory textbook provided students with a statement of opinion disguised as fact: "Votes are decisive politically: they determine which people hold most of the key authoritative offices. Rarely in political science do we find this happy combination of readily available quantified data and obvious political significance. Votes are counted and votes count."[18] In a similar vein, Charles Cnudde and Deane Neubauer explain: "The voting process has received more attention by political analysts than any other feature of the democratic process . . . because of the intrinsic importance of the voting act."[19] Childhood patterns of socialization emphasize elections and voting as primary forms of political activity. Robert Weissberg concludes: "There is, especially among older children, an awareness of non-electoral forms of political participation, but in no way do these rival voting and elections as appropriate channels of citizen political power."[20]

Within this democracy-as-elections framework, political parties have been regarded, as in the British model, as critical and vital linkage institutions providing the primary means of ensuring popular influence and control. Ernest Barker, an eminent British political scientist, counseled that in a representative democracy people ought to participate through parties, whose business it was to define issues and nominate candidates pledged to the party platform.[21] In the United States, E. E. Schattschneider gave voice to this same ideal in 1942, when he wrote, "Political parties created democracy and . . . modern democracy is unthinkable save in terms of parties."[22] Some years later, as a member of the American Political Science Association panel on political parties, Schattschneider and his colleagues chose to downplay American constitutional realities and issue a report that urged adoption of a party system which "must be democratic, responsible and effective" and patterned after the British party system they so admired.[23] John Saloma and Frederick Sontag echoed this confidence in parties more recently when they claimed, "Political parties . . . offer the best potential means of achieving broad citizen participation in politics and continuing citizen influence in the direction of government."[24]

On the revisionist side, the existence of meaningful elections operating through competing parties has become the litmus test for determining whether a political democracy exists. C. Wright Mills embodies this assumption with a critical observation:

In [the classic] image of elections the people are presented with problems. They discuss them. They formulate viewpoints. These viewpoints are organized and they compete. One viewpoint "wins out." Then the people act on this view, or their representatives are instructed to act it out and this they promptly do. Such are the images of democracy which are still used.[25]

This general acceptance of the assumption that political democracy is necessarily electoral has created an intellectual trap, particularly for the consensus school, because attempts to measure the operative realities of American politics against the normative standards of representative democracy has left unbridgeable intellectual gaps. It has become less and less possible to ignore the reality that the electoral process is in progressive disarray and that political parties are in a state of terminal decline. Moreover, if we assume that elections and voting are of critical importance, it remains a mystery why American voters—considerably better fed, better educated, and more affluent than their counterparts elsewhere in the world—vote irrationally. Under these circumstances, and working within the presumption that elections, hence parties, are vital to democracy, the question "Is American democracy viable?" is being asked increasingly.

The revisionists have long professed their doubts on this point. Kenneth Prewitt and Alan Stone note the absence of electoral accountability:

Even a cursory comparison between this picture [of how representative democracy ought to function] and the way in which election campaigns are conducted will reveal a yawning chasm indeed. . . . It is often not a system whereby candidates are held accountable for their actions, but rather one in which there is frequently no accountability for political actions.[26]

Such revisionist doubts are beginning to spread into the consensus camp. Pomper now fears that the "ultimate cost of the decline of parties is the loss of popular control over public policies."[27] This fear takes on added significance because there appears to be no groundswell of public support for repairing the electoral process by reviving political parties. In 1966, Jack Dennis uncovered popular ambivalence toward political parties which is clear from the responses he obtained to the statement "The best rule in voting is to pick the man regardless of his party." A substantial number (82 percent) either agreed or agreed strongly. On another statement, "The parties do more to confuse the issues than to provide a clear choice on them," 54 percent agreed.[28] Decades later public esteem for parties remains low.

The United States: A "Citizen-Participant" Democracy

The structural conditions of the American political system, as well as its culture, contradict the assumptions of normative democratic theory. Ernest

Barker, for example, had assumed the presence of two related conditions for a representative form of democracy to flourish: strong national political parties working within a parliamentary form of government dominated by a cabinet.[29] It is doubtful whether a presidential system burdened with fragmented state and local institutions (the federal system) is capable of providing the institutional infrastructure that must exist to support a "responsible" party system. As a practical matter, the implementation of representative "democracy" in a federal system had resulted in a multiplicity of elective offices, which only compounded the vitiation of party responsibility by making it impossible to create a national organization that could be centrally controlled. The absence of party discipline, together with so many elective offices, ironically has led to a political system especially susceptible to middle-class mass nonelectoral penetration, one in which individual legislators could be swayed by public pressures after an election was over. In such a system, representative democracy as conceived by British theorists is almost impossible to establish.

Moreover, aside from the consequences of institutional form, it is doubtful whether Americans are prepared to accept a truly representative type of democracy, which entails limitations on popular influence by confining the people to voting on candidates chosen for them by political parties. Historically the very idea of "democracy" in the United States—which resulted in the "democratization" of political parties—entailed more, not less, public influence in the kinds of things parties were traditionally supposed to do, namely, choose candidates and construct a platform to which representatives would be bound, both before and after the election.

Looking at the other side of the cultural coin, Americans have not shown any signs of wanting what representative democracy inevitably produces—majority rule. Indeed, the opportunities to thwart majority rule and protect minority interests were built into the system from its inception, the filibuster in the Senate being one example. Attempts to amend Senate rules and make it easier to cut off debate have been consistently rebuffed. One such attempt in the 1950s impelled Walter Lippmann to remind the public that "the American idea of a democratic decision has always been that important minorities must not be coerced.... The right of unlimited debates is merely a device, rather an awkward and tiresome device, to prevent large and determined communities from being coerced."[30]

When minority rights cannot be achieved through the electoral process they have traditionally and increasingly found protection outside of it, particularly through the courts. As Richard Rose observes, "Time and again the Court has upheld claims of individuals, as against the collective weight of a government elected by a majority."[31] For example, until the 1950s electoral legislation in the Deep South and elsewhere deprived black citizens of their rights. Represented by middle-class pressure groups like the NAACP, minorities entered the federal courts and asked to have such practices as segregation, which had been endorsed repeatedly by a majority of voters in their home states, declared illegal. The same has been true of the rights of criminals.[32]

These realities make it essential to reconsider the present nature and form of American democracy. It can be more appropriately characterized not as "representative" but as "citizen-participant." At the same time that elections have receded in importance, alternative procedural mechanisms through which citizens can exert influence and exercise control have taken their place.[33] Public participation is not limited to elections, as in other representative forms of democracy, but occurs continuously. Moreover, the system is open enough to admit direct nonelectoral participation at several points in the legislative, administrative, and judicial process. This penetrability sets the United States apart from other nondemocratic regimes in which the absence of meaningful elections is not compensated for by the presence of similar alternative extra-electoral channels. In addition, the operation of checks and balances works alongside and in many instances has replaced the electoral sanction as a means of ensuring the imposition of popular control. In other words, public control and influence exist, but outside the electoral process. In the Soviet Union, though participation may be more extensive than in the United States, much of that activity is involuntary and does not necessarily produce significant responsiveness on the part of decision-makers.[34] The United States, then, is a democracy not because it has meaningful elections but *even though it does not.*

Can Nonelectoral Policy-making Be Curtailed?

Despite the weakening of the institutional and organizational underpinnings of representative democracy, we have argued that American democracy is viable, though nonrepresentative in character. This analysis is a pragmatic not a judgmental one. Nevertheless, the primacy of the nonelected branches has not been without its critics, and plans are afoot to reassert the political prerogatives of the elected branches. We will briefly consider whether these efforts are likely to succeed.

Even if the cultural, institutional, and organizational realities of American politics, which we have discussed in this chapter, could be changed, other developmental realities suggest future failure. Indeed, efforts under the Reagan administration, particularly, have not been focused on the repair of political parties, whose organizational decay seems almost beyond repair, or on attempts to defractionalize the institutional structure. More and more federal laws are destined for implementation at the state and local levels, especially if the block grant concept becomes entrenched. Hence the focus of current efforts has been directed at curtailing "judicial activism" and "bureaucratic rule-making."

Efforts at remediation assume that replacing U.S. Supreme Court justices with ones likely to practice "restraint" will be sufficient to curtail activism. Leaving aside the practical question of whether it is possible to predict future judicial performance (witness the rulings of Hugo Black and Earl Warren on the bench), will replacement of Supreme Court justices as vacancies occur produce judicial restraint?

Moreover, the U.S. Supreme Court has original jurisdiction in only a few cases, with the lower federal courts and regional appeals courts doing much of the judicial reshaping.[35] The role of the Supreme Court has been merely to rule on whether the lower courts acted within their authority. In the matter of forced school busing to achieve integration, the original ruling was made by a lower federal court. Even in cases where the Supreme Court has made new law by overturning lower court rulings (which it has done in only a few instances), the Supreme Court could not have acted without the action of the lower courts. That being the case, presidents are less able to control appointments throughout the large federal judiciary, even though technically all judicial appointments require presidential approval. Nominations tend to originate with state political leaders and senior senators and require only pro forma presidential approval. It would require a denial of precedent and of senatorial courtesies to change this.

As we have seen, judicial activism has been foisted on the judiciary as a result of the growth in administrative rule-making, while the Supreme Court's actions on social issues are, in major part, due to a lack of congressional will and ability to resolve difficult questions through the machinery of electoral politics. These are the underlying trends, and they are not amenable to easy control, even by determined Chief Executives. One case in point involved the Internal Revenue Service (IRS), which interpreted the congressional mandate given it by denying tax exemptions to private and religious schools that practice racial discrimination. Despite President Ronald Reagan's attempt to place the matter on the congressional agenda by sending Congress a bill authorizing the IRS to so act, Congress chose to shelve the matter. Instead, Bob Jones University, the party affected by the IRS ruling, took the matter to court. In May 1983 the U.S. Supreme Court handed down a verdict that upheld the IRS.[36] Thus, despite President Reagan's past ire at "attempts to enforce a judicial resolution of political and public policy issues properly left to the electorate,"[37] the lack of congressional will to act on this matter left the judiciary, not Congress, in charge of ruling on an administrative action that affects social policy.

Attempts to rein in bureaucratic rule-making activity are also likely to end in failure. Given the congressional imperative to gain reelection at the expense of all other goals, attention to political survival often results in vague legislative mandates requiring bureaucratic interpretation. We cannot count on "sunset laws," which require regulatory agencies to justify their existence, to curtail bureaucratic growth. The experience of the thirty-four states that have enacted such laws since Colorado pioneered them in 1976 is instructive. Few laws have been taken off the books; few agencies have been cut back. Bureaucratic oversight is tedious and an unwise allocation of legislative time, given the lack of public attention it attracts and the scant political mileage it generates.[38]

Another measure intended to reassert congressional power is the "legislative veto," which consists of legislative language that can be attached to bills, allowing Congress to review the rules and regulations promulgated by executive agencies. This bill failed to pass the House by the required two-thirds majority in 1976 and was vetoed by President Gerald Ford when attached as a rider to a pesticides control bill. More recently (1980), however, the House tried again by voting an amendment to a bill (to extend the Environmental Protection Agency's programs to fiscal year 1981) that would enable Congress to veto any pesticide regulations promulgated by the agency if they were found to be objectionable to the constituents of certain legislators.[39] Also in 1980, Congress reserved the right to veto, with the consent of both houses, new Federal Trade Commission regulations. The legislative veto is included in more than one hundred federal laws.

The legislative veto, however, met with strenuous opposition from the Reagan administration, which contended that it was unconstitutional if it intruded on the President's power to manage the executive branch. The Reagan administration's position was tested in the U.S. Supreme Court in a case involving an immigration law that contained a provision authorizing either the Senate or the House to veto certain rulings by the attorney general.

The Court ruled on June 23, 1983, that the legislative veto was unconstitutional because it clashed with the constitutionally designated allocation of powers between the legislative and executive branches of government.

Neither the sunset laws nor the legislative veto addresses the problem that is the cause of the lack of congressional control—Congress's own lack of discipline and cohesion and its unwillingness to take stands and make authoritative choices on political issues. Until Congress recaptures its political authority (and it is unlikely to do so without the discipline imposed by strong political parties), the sharing of decision-making power with both the bureaucracy and the courts is likely to continue.

If Congress cannot act to curb the bureaucracy, the question remains whether a determined President can tame bureaucratic decision-making. The most determined of recent presidents has been Ronald Reagan, and the record is far from clear. While his administration has undoubtedly had an impact on the quantity of rule-making, it has yet to draw up a consistent plan to tighten the statutory mandates of agencies to regulate, undoubtedly because the matter would stir up a political hornet's nest. Indeed, ironically, the bill sent to Congress by President Reagan on the matter of the IRS ruling on tax exemptions would have authorized a further delegation of congressional authority to a government agency (by seeking to give the IRS explicit legislative power to deny tax-exempt status to schools that discriminate) instead of a bill that would have specified legislative guidelines to administrative agencies to limit their statutory authority.

The actions taken by the Reagan administration to curtail bureaucratic rule-making are transient enough that they can be altered by a new administration. They have included proposals to underfund and/or disband agencies; the issuing of an executive order giving the Office of Management and Budget power to review executive agency rules; the setting up of the Presidential Task Force on Regulatory Relief; and the appointment as agency heads of persons who sympathize with the administration's goal of reducing federal regulation. Not only are these measures temporary, but their effectiveness in achieving administration goals has been stymied by organized pressure groups on many fronts.

Consider the matter of underfunding of certain agencies. The Federal Trade Commission and the Consumer Product Safety Commission, two independent consumer-oriented agencies, were early targets. In the case of the latter agency, plans to disband it or alternatively transfer it to the Commerce Department were overruled, while extensive budget-cutting of both agencies proved unacceptable to congressional supporters. The underfunding of other agencies, such as the Environmental Protection Agency (whose budget was reduced in 1982 to $1.391 billion from $1.426 billion in 1981) must be seen in the context of a huge and unsustainable explosion of EPA funding which had taken place during the previous decade (from $71 million in 1970 to $1.426 billion in 1981).[40]

The results of another Reagan administration tactic to curb and control agency rule-making through the appointments process have been equivocal at best. Some regulatory heads have curtailed the regulatory activities of the agencies they head; for example, under James Miller, head of the Federal Trade Commission, the free market will be allowed to work out many consumer protection and antitrust problems that would have been regulated in the past. Yet other regulatory agencies with new appointees sympathetic to Reagan administration goals have not been as successful. Under the tenure of Anne Gorsuch Burford as head of the EPA, the goal of substantially easing environmental controls on industry was frequently blocked by widespread public and congressional opposition. Opponents did not want to see a rollback of antipollution laws and regulations recently developed.[41] In large part because of such hostility, the EPA in mid-1981 hastily withdrew a package of proposed changes to the Clean Air Act intended to loosen the law on environmental regulation. Other efforts by the EPA to change agency rules in order to provide regulatory relief to industry attracted so much controversy that they too were withdrawn. Environmental interest groups such as the Natural Resources Defense Council, the Environmental Defense Fund, the Sierra Club, the Legal Defense Fund, and the National Wildlife Federation have actively filed lawsuits to block rules deemed obnoxious to the spirit of the Clean Air Act[42] (sixteen legal actions were filed in 1981). Gorsuch's replacement at the EPA, William Ruckelshaus, early conceded the impact of environmental public interest groups on the agency and indicated that pollution laws would not (and indeed because of congressional pressure could not) be eased and would probably be made even more stringent.[43]

Other agencies, primarily those engaged in economic regulation have maintained, if not increased, their regulatory activities. For instance, the Interstate Commerce Commission, under Reese H. Taylor, Jr., reasserted some controls over the trucking industry, particularly with respect to the granting of new routes to trucking companies.

The Reagan administration, having opposed the legislative veto as a means of checking bureaucratic rule-making, has instituted an alternative means of control. By Executive Order 12291 (issued in February 1981), the Office of Management and Budget (OMB) was given the power to review executive agency rules and to order agencies to hold up publishing proposed rules until their plans could be reviewed by the OMB. The latter's own performance was to be monitored by a "Presidential Task Force on Regulatory Relief." The principles guiding the OMB were:

1. Federal regulations should be initiated only when there is a compelling need.
2. Alternative regulatory approaches (e.g., no regulation) should be considered and the approach selected that imposes the least possible burdens on societies consistent with achieving the overall statutory and policy objectives.
3. Regulatory priorities should be governed by an assessment of the benefits and costs of the proposed regulations.[44]

Because the Reagan administration has avoided seeking permanent changes in the statutory authority of regulatory agencies, no real reform has taken place, even though OMB oversight may curb some of the excesses of bureaucratic rule-making. The executive order covers only rules issued by executive branch agencies, and not rules issued by independent regulatory agencies. In addition, specific parts of the order—notably that cost-benefit analysis be applied to agency rules—are difficult to apply, especially to rules issued by agencies engaged in social regulation, where specific benefits are not easily quantifiable. Ironically, despite the Reagan administration's distaste for judicial intervention, the U.S. Supreme Court ruled against the use of cost-benefit analysis by the Occupational Safety and Health Administration in a case involving workers' exposure to cotton dust, suggesting instead the standard of "cost-effectiveness."[45]

It appears that for the foreseeable future the electoral branches will only minimally be able to reassert control over extra-electoral decision-makers—the courts and the bureaucracy.

Elections as Rituals

We have been arguing that elections in the United States have become largely ritualistic events with only vestigial instrumental significance. Nevertheless, elections remain an important part of the nation's legitimizing myth. Dan Nimmo and James Combs have defined myth as "the taken for granted set of assumptions, conceptions and ideas that lie below the threshold of consciousness . . . that substantial realm of dramatic accounts whose accuracy and plausibility go largely unquestioned."[46] The deep-seated nature of political myth, reinforced by socialization, ensures that elections will continue to play a profound subliminal role in American politics. Moreover, conformity to the myth by politically relevant members who engage in electoral participation serves several important purposes, which combine to maintain the stability of the political order.

Elections, and voting, have a tension-relieving, politically cathartic function. The emotionally charged atmosphere in which such contests are conducted contrasts with the daily operations of government and of instrumental political activity, which are "detailed, complex, mundane [and] virtually colorless."[47] Even though engaging in such activities yields tangible benefits, citizens cannot be expected to live by bread alone. Taking part in activity that is immediately satisfying, even if it serves minimal tangible political purposes, enables citizens to return with equanimity to the humdrum (if materially rewarding) routines of their daily lives.

From the perspective that our elections have turned primarily into political rituals, it is interesting to note that they have throughout history been "spectacles" replete with the appropriate festive paraphernalia of balloons, bands, beer, hats, music, flags, parades, and processions. It is no accident that we are able to refer to the "bandwagon" effect, a term not used in connection with elections anywhere else in the world. Little wonder that Almond and Verba reported that the reason most people gave for voting was "the sense of gratification" it provided.[48] As if compensating for their lack of substance, our elections are growing more expensive, more colorful, and more lengthy each year. By way of contrast, British elections, which are of far greater instrumental significance, are brief and virtually colorless. Nowhere is the cliché that size and style bear an inverse relationship to the importance of an event more clearly borne out than at the quadrennial national conventions in the United States. They are growing more swollen and garish at the same time that presidential primaries are increasing in number, thereby robbing the conventions of their ostensible purpose—to choose the presidential candidate. What the convention does, increasingly, is ratify the popular choice as revealed in the primaries, but there would undoubtedly be a national outcry if it were to be suggested that conventions be abolished.

Elections also serve as a forum for expression, and reinforcement, of regime support which in the United States is given by the politically relevant segments of the community. David Easton reminds us that regular demonstrations of support are vital in maintaining a sense of political cohesion and community.[49] The shared understandings by means of which any community survives are exceedingly fragile and in need of periodic reinforcement. Voting—a highly dramatic, disciplined, and repetitive act—serves to create and maintain a sense of national solidarity and community and to reinforce the bonds of togetherness. Thus even when it is devoid of any instrumental purpose, voting is crucially valuable in and of itself.

That sense of political cohesion produced by the common experience of voting is heightened by the use of appropriate political symbols during the course of the election. As in other rituals, these symbols serve to dramatize the occasion. The political equivalents of the Christmas tree or the Easter egg are the American flag and the conspicuous references to national icons or "things revered," such as The Family, The Constitution, Great Public Heroes, or key ideological catch phrases like "free enterprise." Such symbols serve to "arouse admiration and enthusiasm, setting forth and strengthening faiths and loyalties. They not only arouse emotions indulgent of the social structure but also heighten awareness of the sharing of these emotions by others, thereby promoting mutual identification and providing a basis for solidarity."[50] In a diverse nation such as the United States, symbols provide a kind of social glue. In fact, some of the most successful political campaigns have been conducted on a highly abstract symbolic level and have avoided specific issues and detailed commitments. A case in point was the highly successful "politics of love" motif of Jimmy Carter's presidential quest in 1976, in which Carter-as-candidate promised to restore to us a government as good as its people, a promise made necessary by the political corruption unearthed by the Watergate affair but not carried out.

Elections also serve to imbue our elected decision-makers with legitimacy. This "democratic coronation" function is considered a prerequisite for the successful exercise of power, the means by which it is converted into authority. In fact, elections provide a unique opportunity for citizens to become accustomed to accept their equals as masters—something Rousseau suggested was necessary before the people would permit their equals to exercise power over them. American elections, even more than those elsewhere, are occasions during which otherwise remote decision-makers are forced to come out into the open (often literally) and to engage in daily activities with the rest of us. They are forced to kiss our babies, sample an array of foods, and engage in dialogues, however trivial, with us. Thus reassured of their concern, we agree to bestow on them the cloak of legitimacy and by voting convert our equals into our masters. Moreover in a system in which other decision-makers are not elected—bureaucrats and judges being either faceless or remote—the legitimacy accorded a portion of our decision-makers through the act of voting takes on added significance.

To the functions of legitimation, support generation, and catharsis, we can add the function of political education. That voting could be an educational experience in and of itself is an argument of philosophers as diverse as Aristotle, Rousseau, and John Stuart Mill. L. A. Scaff maintains that in the Aristotelian language of politics, participation in such common political acts engenders feelings of commonality, fraternity, and communication in public relationships.[51] Thus, instead of being an exercise of purely legal rights, they become an affirmation of belonging. For Rousseau, participation and citizenship were coterminous, the entire electoral experience being one through which the citizen became socialized.[52] This communal and public feature of electoral participation was emphasized also by John Stuart Mill, who considered it a means by which a citizen's horizons could be broadened and without which a citizen would become trapped in a narrowly privatized existence.[53]

There is some empirical evidence to suggest that elections, by providing common experiences for those who choose to participate in them, do reinforce support for the regime, if not shared conceptions of the public good. For example, a recent study by Benjamin Ginsberg and Robert Weissberg found that while voters undergo attitudinal shifts favorable to the regime after the election, this changeover effect appears to be less evident among nonvoters. Basing their analyses of election-related attitudinal changes on data collected by the Survey Research Center on the 1968 and 1972 presidential elections, they discovered that the clearest impact of these elections was in the area of regime support. After both elections, the regime was perceived as more responsive, more capable, and more honest by those who had voted, and less so by those who had abstained. For example, in 1972 the difference between voters and nonvoters was particularly striking on the question of whether respondents thought that public officials "cared" (about people like themselves). The authors noted that among voters a sizable proportion of those who prior to the election thought that officials did not care offered a more positive appraisal after the election. By the same token, they add, those who did not vote became more negative on this score. Changes in "popular trust and confidence in government" measures were similarly dramatic. In the 1972 election, on questions measuring the capability of government, among Nixon voters 41 percent of respondents with negative preelection perceptions became positive after the election. Moreover, about the same number (41.1 percent) also thought the government more honest.[54]

It is through electoral participation that those who gain most from the system sustain, nourish, and preserve the myth that the United States *is* a functioning representative democracy even when the operative realities suggest otherwise. It is unlikely that this is done intentionally, to deflect the energies of the have-nots into such noninstrumental and largely symbolic activities as voting, thereby to limit the numbers of those engaging in more instrumentally meaningful activities. More likely, the middle-class commitment to voting and elections, reinforced through childhood socialization, reflects a normative belief that since they *ought* to be important events they *are* vital components in a democracy. Elections still serve as the standard by which we measure the existence of political democracy elsewhere. When we label another nation "undemocratic," it is either because elections do not exist or because they have no instrumental meaning.

Whatever the abstract commitments of Americans, the necessity of voting in elections seems to have become a convenient political fiction to which all Americans pay lip service but which not all practice. This intellectual commitment to the electoral process is reflected in the habitual *overreporting* of electoral participation. In only one, perhaps two, other areas are people likely to be as disingenuous! Moreover, the fact that far fewer people actually vote than claim to have voted, plus the fact that those who do vote are the ones who obtain their instrumental benefits elsewhere and by other means, puts the institution of elections in much the same category as the institution of marriage for socially prominent but promiscuous Victorians in the nineteenth century. Those who have the greatest stake in any society want to preserve the status quo and will do so by perpetuating society's myths (i.e., normative ideals) even while they take advantage of its realities.

The Role of Elections in a "Citizen-Participant" Democracy

Even at this stage it will be helpful to restate what our purpose has been. We have engaged in a frank attempt to reinterpret, reevaluate, and analyze the evidentiary materials *at hand*. As informed observers well know, decades of empirical research on the subject of voting behavior and other forms of political participation have accumulated. The question now must be: "What are we to make of it all?" This more than anything else has been the impetus for and focus of our effort. Substantiation of the thesis presented, through in-depth empirical testing, can and should be left to others. It is beyond the scope of this book. What is offered readers is an interpretation of the role of voting in American politics which looks at the effects of developmental changes both within *and outside* the electoral process, an interpretation strongly supported by the circumstantial evidence.

Not only have we characterized voting as ritualistic and elections as symbolic, we have also described American democracy as "citizen-participant" rather than representative in character. Only from this perspective can the unique symbolic role of American elections (as opposed to those in other democratic regimes) become understandable. Within this type of democracy, elections constitute the *last* step in the democratic process, their function being primarily one of legitimation. In contrast, in other more familiar representative democracies elections are crucial events, the *first* step in the democratic process.

In the United States, however, voting is preceded by other nonelectoral participatory activities that serve to maintain and extend popular influence and control. We have added the caveat that while there are no structural impediments to such modes of participation, the system is sufficiently complex to favor citizens who possess political sophistication and technical expertise and can thus participate in a policy-making process that for the most part proceeds outside the electoral process through the extra-electoral channels of administrative and judicial action. It is hardly surprising under such circumstances that participants in the political system are more likely to be drawn from the middle-class "haves." The broad mass of Americans, however, are middle-class, if not by income then by temperament. And so we return to the hypothesis stated at the beginning—that it is the beneficiaries of the political system who make a rational choice to give the system their symbolic support by voting, while those who are disadvantageously situated make an equally rational choice to stay away.

Notes

1. Jack Dennis, "Support for the Institution of Elections by the Mass Public," *American Political Science Review* 64 (September 1970): 819.
2. Austin Ranney and Wilmore Kendall have defined political democracy as "simply and solely a way of making decisions, and the *content* of any particular decision (except insofar as it affects the nature of the decision-making *process*) is irrelevant to the presence or absence of democracy." See "Basic Principles for a Modern Democracy" in *Empirical Democratic Theory*, ed. Charles Cnudde and Deane Neubauer (Chicago: Markham Publishing Co., 1969), p. 60. Emphasis in the original.

3. See Peter Bachrach, *The Theory of Democratic Elitism: A Critique* (Boston: Little, Brown & Co., 1967), p. 18n.
4. Joseph Schumpeter, *Capitalism, Socialism, and Democracy* (New York: Harper & Row, 1942), p. 250.
5. A. D. Lindsay, *The Modern Democratic State,* vol. 1 (London: Oxford University Press, 1947), p. 284.
6. Ibid., p. 25.
7. C. B. McPherson, *The Real World of Democracy* (New York: Oxford University Press, 1975), p. 8. Emphasis added.
8. Dorothy Pickles, *Democracy* (New York: Basic Books, 1970), p. 13. Emphasis added.
9. J. Roland Pennock, *Democratic Political Theory* (Princeton: Princeton University Press, 1979), p. 7.
10. Robert M. MacIver, *The Ramparts We Guard* (New York: Macmillan Co., 1950), p. 27.
11. Robert Dahl, *Polyarchy* (New Haven: Yale University Press, 1971), p. 3.
12. Anthony Downs, *An Economic Theory of Democracy* (New York: Harper & Row, 1957), pp. 23–24.
13. Seymour Martin Lipset, *Political Man* (Garden City, N.Y.: Doubleday & Co., 1960), p. 27.
14. Deane Neubauer, "Some Conditions of Democracy," in *Empirical Democratic Theory,* ed. Cnudde and Neubauer, p. 227. See also R. N. Jackman, "Political Democracy and Social Equality: A Comparative Analysis," *American Sociological Review* 39 (February 1974): 29–45.
15. Dennis F. Thompson, *The Democratic Citizen* (New York: Columbia University Press, 1970), p. 53. Emphasis added.
16. Gerald Pomper, "The Decline of the Party in American Elections," *Political Science Quarterly* 92 (Spring 1977): 21.
17. Gerald Pomper, *Elections in America* (New York: Dodd, Mead & Co., 1968), p. x.
18. James D. Barber, *Citizen-Politics: An Introduction to Political Behavior* (Chicago: Markham Publishing Co., 1969), p. 3.
19. Cnudde and Neubauer in *Empirical Democratic Theory,* p. 65.
20. Robert Weissberg, *Political Learning, Political Choice, and Democratic Citizenship* (Englewood Cliffs, N.J.: Prentice-Hall, 1974), pp. 66–67.
21. Ernest Barker, *Essays on Government,* 2d edition (Oxford: Clarendon Press, 1951), p. 69.
22. E. E. Schattschneider, *Party Government* (New York: Farrah & Rinehart, 1942), p. 42.

23. See "Towards a More Responsible Two-party System," *American Political Science Review* 44 (1950): 1.
24. John Saloma and Frederick Sontag, *Parties: The Real Opportunity for Effective Citizen Politics* (New York: Alfred A. Knopf, 1972), p. x.
25. C. Wright Mills, quoted in *Power, Politics, and People: The Collected Essays of C. Wright Mills,* ed. Irving Horowitz (New York: Oxford University Press, 1963).
26. Kenneth Prewitt and Alan Stone, *The Ruling Elite: Elite Theory and Power in American Democracy* (New York: Harper & Row, 1973), p. 204.
27. See Pomper, "The Decline of the Party," p. 41.
28. Jack Dennis, "Support for the Party System by the Mass Public," *American Political Science Review* 60 (September 1966): 605.
29. Barker, *Essays on Government,* p. 69.
30. Walter Lippman, quoted in *New York Herald Tribune,* March 3, 1949. See also Austin Ranney, "Towards a More Responsible Two-party System: A Commentary," *American Political Science Review* 45 (June 1951): 488–99.
31. Richard Rose, in Guy Hermet, Richard Rose, and Alain Rocquie, eds., *Elections Without Choice* (New York: John Wiley & Sons, 1978), p. 200.
32. A similar view has been proposed by Roger W. Cobb and Charles D. Elder, *Participation in American Politics* (Boston: Allyn & Bacon, 1972), p. 162.
33. See also Sidney Verba and Norman Nie, *Participation in America: Political Democracy and Social Equality* (New York: Harper & Row, 1972), p. 44. See also Lester Milbrath and M. L. Goel, *Political Participation* (Chicago: Rand McNally & Co., 1977), p. viii.
34. D. Richard Little, "Mass Political Participation in the U.S. and U.S.S.R.: A Conceptual Analysis," *Comparative Political Studies* 8 (January 1976): 442.
35. See Vernon Royster, "Thinking Things Over," *Wall Street Journal,* August 19, 1981, p. 21.
36. *Wall Street Journal,* May 26, 1983, p. 30.
37. *Time,* November 23, 1981, p. 62.
38. *Wall Street Journal,* August 19, 1981, p. 18.
39. *Wall Street Journal,* July 25, 1981, p. 1.
40. *National Journal,* May 15, 1981, p. 1467.
41. See *Wall Street Journal,* February 18, 1983, p. 1.
42. *National Journal,* December 19, 1981, p. 2233.
43. *Wall Street Journal,* June 2, 1983, p. 2.
44. *National Journal,* February 21, 1981, p. 299.
45. *Wall Street Journal,* July 7, 1981, p. 1.
46. Dan Nimmo and James E. Combs, *Subliminal Politics: Myth and Myth Makers in America* (Englewood Cliffs, N.J.: Prentice-Hall, 1981), p. xii.

47. H. Mark Roelofs, *Ideology and Myth in American Politics* (Boston: Little, Brown & Co., 1976), p. 39.
48. See Gabriel Almond and Sidney Verba, *The Civic Culture* (Princeton: Princeton University Press, 1963), p. 146 (see table 13) and p. 15 (see table 15).
49. David Easton, *The Political System* (New York: John Wiley & Sons, 1965), p. 157.
50. Harold Lasswell et al., *The Language of Politics* (Cambridge: M.I.T. Press, 1949), p. 11.
51. L. A. Scaff, "Two Concepts of Political Participation," *Western Political Quarterly* 28 (September 1975): 447–62.
52. Jean Jacques Rousseau, *Political Writings*, ed. C. E. Vaughan (New York: John Wiley & Sons, 1962).
53. See John Stuart Mill, "Representative Government," in *Three Essays* (London: Oxford University Press, 1966), p. 274.
54. See Benjamin Ginsberg and Robert Weissberg, "Elections and the Mobilization of Popular Support," *American Journal of Political Science* 22 (February 1978): 39–41; and "Elections as Legitimizing Institutions" in *Parties and Elections in an Anti-Party Age* (Bloomington: Indiana University Press, 1978).

INDEX

References to figures, notes, or tables are indicated by *f, n,* or *t* following the page number.

Abscam bribery scandal, 25, 38
Administrative Procedures Act of 1946, 8, 67–68, 73–74
airlines industry, regulation of, 54-55, 57
allegiance and alienation, studies of, 103–4
Anderson, John, 33–35
Aristotle, 125
artificial sweeteners, ban on, 58, 69
auto industry, regulation of, 57, 58

banking, regulation of, 61
Bayh, Birch, 36, 48
Bob Jones University, 79n.36, 120
bureaucracy, growth of, 7–8, 53–58
Burford, Anne Gorsuch, 122
Butz, Earl, 50
Byrne, Jane, 25

campaign funds, 3, 26, 101t
candidates: image of, 3, 17, 18–23, 31–33; issue candidates, 33–35; party recruitment of, 3, 25; spending limitations for, 26
Carter, Jimmy: bureaucracy, expansion of, 51; oil price controls, 46–47; presidential campaign, 25–26, 32–33, 125; public confidence in, 53; reelection defeat, 36; urban policy speech, 12
Church, Frank, 36
citizen groups. *See* political action committees
"citizen participant democracy," 13–14, 72, 116–18, 127–28
civic duty, sense of, 98–100
class bias. *See* economic status
Clean Air Act of 1970, 61–62
Common Cause, 67, 68
Con Edison, 74
Conable, Barber, 50
congress: initiators of legislation, 47–49; judicial review of, 8–9, 53–54, 58–62,

133

congress (continued)
 119–20; mandating extra-electoral participation, 8, 45, 67–68; overruling the Supreme Court, 75–76; reelection of incumbents, 36–39; role of members, 37–38, 50–51
Constitution, importance of, 72
Consumer Product Safety Commission, 70, 121
courts(s): civil suits filed in district courts, 62, 66f; judicial review of congressional actions, 8–9, 53–54, 58–62, 119–20; minority rights achieved through, 9, 117–18; role of, 53–54

democracy: American conception of, 13, 112, 117; British conception of, 13, 112–17; "citizen participant democracy," 13–14, 72, 116–18, 127–28; definition of, 112–13; models of, 13, 112–18; revisionist view of, 13; role of elections in, 110–28
Democratic party, 30t, 36
Depository Institutions Deregulation Committee, 61
Depression, the, 7, 23–24
Diggs, Charles, 38
Dingell, John, 74
Dooling, John, 60
Douglas, William O., 50

economic issues and voting, 19, 42n.50
economic status: and extra-electoral activity, 10–12, 63, 66–67; and political action committees, 68; and proto-political activity, 12, 84, 104; and public interest law firms, 70; and social responsibility, 10–11, 76–77; and voting, 10–12, 76–77, 84, 103–7
election(s): belief in, 1–2, 10, 17, 45, 97; efficacy of, 94–95, 96t, 97t; interest in, 102t, 103; operational support of, 101t; revisionist view of, 11; role of, 110–11, 114–16, 127–28; symbolic value of, 5, 10–11, 83–84, 95–107, 123–27; of 1932, 23; of 1972, 21; of 1976, 2, 19, 28–30; of 1980, 41n.36

electoral myth, 17, 45, 97, 123, 126
Emergency Price Control Act of 1942, 57
Environmental Protection Agency, 58, 61–62, 70, 121–22
Equal Employment Opportunity Commission, 55–56
equal-time rule, 33
Errichetti, Angelo, 25
extra-electoral participation in government: contacting public officials, 65t, 90–92, 94t; democracy of, 13–14; economic status, and, 10–12, 63, 66–67; mandated by congress, 8, 45, 67–68; public awareness of, 62, 63t, 96t; rationality of, 63

Federal Communications Commission, 33, 56
Federal Power Commission, 74
Federal Register, 54
federal spending, 1976–1982, 78n.24
Federal Trade Commission, 70, 72–73, 121
Flood, Daniel, 38
Florio, James, 25, 78n.21
Food and Drug Administration, 58
Ford, Gerald R., 33, 42n.48, 46
Frankfurter, Felix, 75
Freedom of Information Act, 68, 71–72
Freeman, Orville, 50

Garth, David, 31, 34–35
General Accounting Office, 72, 73, 74
Goldwater, Barry, 32–34
government: efforts to contact officials, 65t, 90–92, 94t; public trust in, 28t, 103, 126; regulation of the market, 7–8. *See also* extra-electoral participation in government
Gramm-Latta bill, 52

"halo effect," 95
haves and have-nots. *See* economic status
Holum, John, 34
Hoover, Herbert, 42n.48
Hyde Amendment, 59–60

income of families, 6f, 87f, 88f
incumbents, reelection of, 17, 18, 35–39
Independent voters, 29–30

Index

inspectors general, role of, 50–51
"instant voter law," 22–23
Internal Revenue Code of 1954, 57–58
Internal Revenue Service, 119–21
irrationality in voting, 1–4, 16–23, 35–39
issue voting, 4, 20–23, 31–35

Johnson, Lyndon B., 2, 32, 46, 49, 52
Jurash, Stephen, 78n.21

Kennedy, Edward M., 25, 32, 41n.36, 48
Kennedy, John F., 25, 32, 46, 53, 55

law firms, public interest, 70–72
legislative veto power, 120
letter-writing, 62, 64f
Lippmann, Walter, 117

McCarthy, Eugene, 33
McClellan, John, 75
McGovern, George, 21, 33–34, 36
majority rule, 13, 15n.18, 117
Mansfield, Mike, 49–50
Marshall, John, 8, 58
media, and political information, 26–27, 33
Miller, James, 121
minorities: blacks, 9, 84, 87–88, 105; and civic duty, 88–100; elderly, and youth, 76, 87, 104–5; non-voting, 3, 11, 84; political education of, 10–12
mis-voting, 22–23

Nader, Ralph, 67, 68, 71
Napolitan, Joe, 31
National Environmental Policy Act, 68, 71
National Industrial Recovery Act, 57
National Resources Defense Council, 70–71
Nixon, Richard M., 21, 32, 46–47, 50, 51
nonvoting, 3, 11, 84
"not-yet-haves," 76, 87, 104–5

Occupational Safety and Health Administration, 8, 58
Office of Management and Budget, 46, 81n.65, 121, 122–23

parties, political. *See* political parties
personality politics, 3, 17, 18–23
political action committees, 26, 36, 67–70
political alienation index, 103–4
political efficacy, sense of, 94–95, 96t, 97t
political information, 17, 26–27, 33, 42n.56
political parties: affiliation with, 27–31; campaign funds, 3, 26; deterioration of, 3, 17–18, 23–35; efficacy of, 29t; history of, 23–35; loyalty to, 28–31, 35–37; platforms, 30–31; popular participation and, 13; public attitude toward, 27–31, 116; recruitment, control of, 3, 25; reforms of, 26; role in a democratic system, 115–16
presidency: initiator of legislation, 46–47, 51–52; reelection of incumbents, 42n.48; responsibility for actions in office, 3; role of, 46–53, 56; veto, 120. *See also individual names of Presidents*
prospective voting, 16, 18–23
Public Advocates, Inc., 70, 72
Public Citizen, Inc., 67, 68
public interest groups. *See* political action committees

race. *See* minorities
rationality in voting, 1–4, 16–23, 35–39, 95–107
Reagan, Ronald, 32–33, 48, 52, 78n.24, 118–23
registration of voters, 9, 11, 22–23, 84, 105–7
Republican party, 30t
retrospective voting, 16–17, 35–39
revisionist views, 4–6, 11, 13
Rhodes, James, 61–62
rioting and violence, 12, 84, 104
Roosevelt, Franklin D., 56
Rousseau, Jean Jacques, 125

Savings Bond Drive of 1979, 72–73
sulfur-dioxide emission controls, 61–62
sunset laws, 120
Sunshine Law, 70

Index

Supreme Court, 8–9, 53–54, 56–62, 75–76, 118–23
surveys of voters, 2, 14n.1, 20–23, 84–107

ticket splitting, 28–31, 35–37
turnout, 102t, 103, 105–7

U.S. League of Savings Associations, 61
U.S. Savings Bond Drive of 1979, 72–73

veto, legislative, 120
voter(s): age of, 87, 89f, 90f, 92f, 99; economic status of, 10–12, 76–77, 84; education of, 85–86, 93f, 99; employment status and, 93t; income of, 86–87, 88f, 99; race of, 87–94; typical American

voter(s) (continued)
voter, 89; young voters, 76, 87, 104–5
voter registration, 9, 11, 22–23, 84, 105–7
voting: benefits gained by, 11, 17; efficacy of, 94–95, 96t, 97t; irrationality in, 1–4, 16–23, 35–39; issue voting, 4, 20–23, 31–35; mis-voting, 22–23; party affiliation and, 27–31; prospective, 16–17, 18–23; race and, 9, 12, 76, 84, 87–94; rate of, 2, 11–12, 127; reasons for, 95–107; retrospective, 16–17, 35–39; revisionist view of, 4–6; ritualism of, 83–84, 95–107, 123–27; ticket splitting, 28–31, 35–37
Voting Rights Act of 1965, 2, 9

young voters, 76, 87, 104–5

LIBRARY COLLEGE

Books on regula